AF408831

"BREATHING, SLEEP, MEDITATION"

Author: Darien Ma

"BREATHING, SLEEP, MEDITATION"
First book from "**Woman Elevate**" series.
Author: Darien Ma

Copyright © 2023 Darien Ma
All Rights Reserved

This book is for information purposes only. Treat it as such.
The information in this book is not a substitute for the advice, opinion, or assessment of a specialist, physician, or professional. For any problem that arises in your life, seek professional advice. The author of the book, the publisher, and the Darien Ma team cannot be held responsible for any decision, act, or consequence resulting from applying any of the information contained in this book to your own life. You, yourself, are 100% responsible for the choices, actions, and results in your life. So, choose wisely.

Cover: DAR8MA Team
Images credit: canva.com
Contact, e-mail: dar8ma@gmail.com

THANK YOU

I am thankful, with very much gratitude, to all the people in my life who have supported me in all that I have accomplished.

I am thankful to my partner, Lyra, for her inspiration and support so that this series of books could come to light.

I am thankful to my family and all my friends who have helped and supported me in my travels through many countries of the world, who have encouraged me so that this information could reach out in the form of these books, to be available for as many people as possible.

I am thankful also to you, the reader of this book, for your patience and openness in reading this book, but most of all, for your boldness and courage to decide to make beneficial changes into your life.

I hope the information contained in this book, and the following ones, will guide you and inspire you to make the right choices toward a life of quality and harmony.

Darien Ma

"The important thing is not to acquire but to discover!

It is not discovering that is important, but how you discover!

The important thing is not how you discover,
but what the discovery changes inside you!

What is important is not what changes within you,
but what is changed in others by the fact that something
has changed inside you!"

- From the Taoist Teachings

Introduction

Have you ever thought that maybe among those "common" daily habits that you often do "mechanically", automatically, "by itself," perhaps there are aspects you do wrong?...

Have you ever thought that maybe those daily habits that you are doing wrong might affect or destroy slowly, little by little, your Health, Youth, Beauty, Life?...

This is a guidebook designed to provide more different information to help you make wiser choices, better suited FOR YOU, and improve your life.

In a fast-paced world, a world where everything has come more like a "fast forward" speed, more and more people forget how to do some of the basic things (daily habits) correctly they do every day. Daily routines, however, when you do them correctly, could help improve your life. Or, doing them wrong could lead to decay and a life of pain and suffering.

Because the actual issues in the world as the current concepts and "trends" are heading people towards a "fast-food life," or a "speedy-life," and because of the pressing needs these days for a different kind of information, one a bit "different," the author, together with the Darien Ma team, (in the light of the teachings and the therapeutic practices originating from Asia, including decades of experience into working with different kind of people), thought that it would be the time to "pass forward" what they have learned and practiced over time. This way to make available a range of information which, put it into practice, could help improve lives. To have more "different" information, which could give you the possibility to get out of the inertia of everyday life habits and your daily "rituals" and also from the inertia of rational thinking... But more important, to give you the possibility to connect more and more with your Soul. To connect more and more with that part of you that represents your connection with the Spirit, the Universe, and the Divine, God.

That is what these books are written for, in a series that includes this book. A series of guidebooks to help women interested in discovering more about WHO they really ARE, beyond the labels, masks, imprints, or outside programming induced by others over time.

Especially **for women (and girls), are these books dedicated.**

There will be also some more books in this series in the future, dedicated particularly to **girls and women**, especially regarding the **couple relationship** aspects. To learn about HOW and what to be aware of when choosing your right couple partner in life. For you to have a harmonious relationship and a better, happy life.

The time of ignorance is over. The times of: "*I didn't know*"... or: "*I thought that maybe*"... are over now.

Nowadays, with the massive advantage of the internet, which is now at your disposal to find out all sorts of information, the excuse: "I didn't know" no longer holds...

Now, the aspects of life and the environment in which we live in are constantly changing. It's up to each one of us to keep up with these changes that are happening around us. **To align ourselves with these rapid changes accordingly**. First, we need to align ourselves with the environment we live in, with Nature, the Planet, and the Universe. At the same time, also we need to fit in with "the times we live in" and "the society we live in."

Now is the right (and necessary) time to **Wake Up to Reality**. But not towards some "Reality" outside of you. Not to a Reality imposed and induced by others. But **to connect to your Inner Reality**, of each one of you. To be connected with your inner, particular, and specific "Truth." To live in and to experience a Reality generated and created by yourself. Not by others outside of you. A Reality in which YOU are the best version of Your-Self.

Only in this way can you Create a Life and a Future that fits YOU. A life in which you are not just a tiny piece in a big system but a life in which you can Develop yourself and Evolve Holistically, each one of you.

Where you may fully enjoy a life that is not just a "bunch of years," from birth to old age, and what might come after. But rather to enjoy a life in an different environment, where you can Learn, Experiment, Develop, Create, and Evolve unconditionally. And all these to be reached and enjoyed on a Holistic level, not just on the limited physical ("3D") level.

To be able to reach and accomplish multiple levels of Consciousness.

First of all, this book (as well all those from this "*Women Elevate*" book series) is not intended to be a "guide" to present you an "absolute truth" or to give you direct solutions or "fixes" to your particular problems and aspects of your life.

(- Even though much of this information here results from the author's own life experiences, self-development, and practice, and also from working with various people over many decades. As well combined with the work of a team of friends, colleagues, and collaborators in life development: psychology, medicine, "personal development," life coaching, and much more...
Especially of those who searched and went deeper into the mysteries of life: spiritual guides and mentors or alternative or holistic medicine therapists).

This "Women Elevate" series of books come to present you perhaps a little bit of "different" information (maybe a little more "non-ordinary" or "non-rational" ones). Information that could give you that inner impulse to start reflecting and meditating on it and about what is happening in your life. But most of all, on what is going on with Your-Self.
A different kind of information to stimulate each of you to start looking for the right "Answers" and "Solutions" for your life (as well outside yourself, but mostly inside yourself). To help you

in this way, to start working more with yourself, each of you, for your development and evolution in life.

Do your own research about the things regarding your life and your lifestyle. Do not take as "truth" anything other people say, promote, or impose on you. No matter who they are.

Even if someone finds some "truth" for their life, it is not necessary to fit your life as well too. So, go and find Your Own Truth for Your Life!

These "guide" books are dedicated to those who want to make a change in their life. To those who believe they CAN and **DESERVE** more for their life. For those who want their lives to improve in many ways. But first and foremost, for their relationship with themselves. With their Inner-Self.

You will be able to find some information, some possible "Landmarks" and Points of View (POV), that I hope will help you have a healthier life. And perhaps, a Happy and Harmonious one too... but this is depending on the Choices you'll make in your life.

You can find here some different information that may be a little disturbing to someone. Especially to those who have no interest in other people knowing specific information about their own lives.

Those whose interests are to create Dependencies, control and manipulate others, and Profit after that from them. Especially from innocent, gullible, and naive girls and women.

The rush and focus of those who are "pulling the strings" (from "behind the curtain") are constantly after PROFIT ($$$).

And their attention and focus is only on satisfying their personal interests.
Therefore, why would you believe that some of these people ($$$ oriented) would care so much about you, your Health, and especially your WELL-BEING?!?....

You better get out of these illusions you have been inoculated with over time as being "Your Reality" as quickly as possible. Especially to extract yourself from those "programming" and "realities" induced in your life as a result of the interests of others (so not for your happiness and a harmonious life).

However, if you are not one of those who want a change in their life (and not one of those who are interested perhaps in learning some more information that could be useful for others around), and you "accidentally" bought this book, (for which I thank you), do yourself something good and don't waste your time and energy on it. Instead, do a good deed for someone, find the right person who deserves it and needs a Change in her life, and give her this book.

Don't expect this book to fit into certain "patterns" you've been taught before. Nor does it come to present you with just some strictly "Rational" information. Because the "Rational" part of your mind it is only half of your brain's capacity and, at most, only half of your true Inner Potential.
But what would the other half be?...

Why do you think that you are educated, as girls and women, all your life to develop your brain and attention mainly on the Logical-Rational (=> "Yang - Masculine") bases and criteria, since these would represent ONLY half of your brain's capacities, at most?!...

Why are you educated to look for answers and solutions to all your problems, relying predominantly on this Logical-Rational capacity, since it represents only at most HALF of your Brain's Potential?...

Why do you think you did NOT learn ANYTHING about: "The Other Half"?... About the "Soul Mate" of your "Logic-Rational Brain"?...

More importantly, why do you think you are NOT educated about HOW you can use the "other half" in your advantage?...

I am talking about the **INTUITIVE** ("**Yin - Feminine**") side.

Perhaps, with the help of this guidebook, as well as the other books in this guidebook collection, you might get some more "different" information, suggestions, or ideas than you have been taught and "educated" with so far (meaning: "Leaded" and "Programmed" in various ways).

You may ask yourself: how much do those "Settings" and "Programming" ("educations" and "school" preparations), mostly Logical-Rational, (which have been accustomed/set to you since childhood), **help you for real into your life, to have a Happy and Harmonious Life**?...

"Do what makes Your Soul shine!"

"Love is the Song of the Soul singing to God"

„If you believe you'll succeed, you'll see the
opportunities...
If you think you'll fail, you'll see the obstacles."
- Wayne W. Dyer

Chapter 1

BREATHING and the Quality of Life

"If your breathing is agitated, your mind becomes restless."
- From The Toltec Teachings

- What is Breathing?...

- What is the connection between Breathing and the quality of your life?...
- Do you know how vital Breathing is for your Health or the well-being of your life?...
- Did you know that "Breathing" is one of the best-kept secrets of living on this Planet?...
- Did you know that Breathing is a form of (primary) Food for your body?...
- How important is Smoking in your life?...
- WHAT "gifts" smoking can bring to your body?
- Did you know that Breathing is one of the most handy methods to control Stress?

Breathing is one of the most essential processes in the body.
It is the body's main source of nourishment for Oxygen and Energy Supply.
On the other hand, Breathing process also helps to remove Toxins from the body. It is the No.1 System for eliminating waste and toxins from the body.
Why do you think Breathing is the Main Source of nourishment for the body?...

Have you ever wondered how many days you could live without eating?... But without drinking anything? A few days, at least.

But about Breathing, how long could you go without breathing? Just a few minutes. WHY?...

Because Breathing is actually the PRIMARY source of nourishment (both physical, but mostly subtle), for each of us, on this Planet, on this "Earth."

In a way, our inner "engine" empowers us in everything we do.

Therefore, **proper Breathing** is the secret to all activities of your life.

Depending on how you Breathe, these activities of yours may or may not be quality ones.

Long, or Short?...

An important aspect related to Breathing: has been observed over time (both in humans and also in various species of animals in Nature): **the more profound and slower ("long") Breathing is, the longer humans live** (as well the animals too).

Ideally, Breathing should be deeper and "Abdominal." This way, your Breathing can Oxygenate and Energize your whole body.

On the other hand, those who breathe quickly, shortly, or intermittently ("Short" Breathing) are people who live a shorter life.

Thus, we can say that:

16

- The "shorter" the Breath is, the shorter the life becomes.
- The "longer" and deeper the Breath, the longer life could be.
And not only that. There is another component: **Quality of Life**. The deeper the Breath, the better the Quality of Life becomes.
Longer Breathing also helps relieve Stress and calm the inner self. As we already know, Stress is a well-known component that helps shorten life and significantly lowering the quality of life. The more stressed people are, the less they enjoy life.

There is a basic rule of the Soul:
- The more and more fully the person enjoys life, the longer and more quality of life becomes;
- The less one enjoys life, the shorter life becomes proportionally.

Also, the more people live a sedentary life without regular sports exercises, which involve breathing in (inhaling) more Oxygen and fresh air (more significant amounts of it), the shorter their lives become, and more importantly, the lower their Quality of Life. They also age faster.
Likewise, the more people live more sedentary lives, the shorter their lives become. And more importantly, the lower their quality of life is. They also age faster. Because the lack of those regular exercises and movements that can involve breathing in more Oxygen and fresh air, which could help them have a different quality of life.
Exercising regularly is very important, but the **ENVIRONMENT** where you practice is equally important.
In order to have an "Oxygen Refresh" consistently, it is essential to exercise, move, and breathe Deep and Slow

"Fresh Air" in Nature. I mean not in polluted areas. But where the **Air you breathe is Fresh and Clean.**
Spending time in Nature helps your Health and also improves your Quality of Life and Well-Being. It can help you be happier.

The lack of Clean and Fresh Air in your life, especially in your lungs and body, leads to **premature Aging**.
Simply breathing in nature and doing some exercises and walks may not be enough... It is essential NOT to do all this "mechanically," "automatically," like a robot.
The most important is to get to **Breathe CONSCIOUSLY** (not "robotic").
And **Consciously**, to be able to **"Connect"** and **Receive** what **Nature** offers you. That is, to align yourself with Nature's energies and benefits.

In addition to the other benefits it offers, Breathing correctly (slower and deeper) helps a lot for the Energy and Vitality of the body.
It is very important to observe and be aware of your **Breathing**.
Mainly, it's **RHYTHM** (at least from time to time).
It is important to observe yourself: when do happen those situations and moments in your life when "irregular" reactions (tendencies of "blocking" or limiting) of your Breathing in the body occur?... Thus, when starts limiting you from having deep and "full" Breathing?...
Which are the moments when your Breath changes suddenly and becomes small (short), fast, and shallow?
Having fast, shortly "gasping," "panting," rapid, and "choked" Breathing is a "sign" a result may occur in the body at times

when it is overworked, "forced," or "turned on" more than "normal." Signs that highlight you that "something" is blocking, restricting, or limiting your body. So Breathing rhythm brings these issues to your attention.

Being too "short," your Breath CANNOT optimally oxygenate your body. Nor can it optimally and efficiently supply it with Energy (with "Prana") either.

You've probably noticed over time that the more you enter into Stressful, "Alert" states, the more "tense," fast, and short your Breath becomes.

These aspects, if they keep repeating constantly or become a daily or a constant "routine" (a "normality"), over time will attract unpleasant effects, both in the body and in your life (as a result of the respective "deficiencies").

But, if you become aware and observe the rhythm of your Breathing, you will discover the moments or situations in your life that are "stressful" or "over-demanding" to you. This way, you'll be able to make the appropriate and proper changes, especially where is necessary. You can eliminate, or approach differently, the specific situations or aspects of your life so they no longer "Stress" or "Over-Demand" your body unnecessarily.

For example, the breathing rate of the inhabitants of big cities (from those urban agglomerations) tends to reach about **17-22 breaths/minute**.

On the other hand, for those who have already started to practice and work with themselves for a while, their rate of Breathing calms down. It becomes slower and deeper, reaching about **7-9 breaths/minute**. This way, the practitioners manage to bring much more Oxygen into their bodies with less effort.

Unfortunately, there are still many people (adults) who do not know how to breathe correctly and healthily.

There have been many cases where adult people, put in the situation of learning to breathe correctly and deeply, in the first phase, they actually could not do it. They actually choked. Cause they had so many blockages inside their bodies. Much quicker children learn how to breathe correctly than adults past a certain age.

A **minimum of 20-30 minutes of physical exercise per day** is highly recommended to practice (but is **a must** also) if you want to live a healthy life. Ideally, you should practice about 60-90 minutes a day.

Also, **Healthy Eating, Breathing exercises, and Energetic practice (like Tai Chi, Qi-Gong, Yoga, etc.) can help you to Balance and develop harmonious inner states**.

Moreover, these practices and breathing exercises can train your body to know how to set yourself and how you can cope, especially when you have to go through more demanding, stressful, or crisis situations.

In general, most people panic or freeze when there are very demanding or major crisis situations they have to go through. One of the body's automatic reaction when going through such crises is to "freeze." The rhythm of Breathing becomes increasingly rapid and short. In this way, the body is deprived of those two major essential components: Oxygen and direct energy supply. Because of this (major) cause, the body then ends up collapsing in a very short time.

Prior training is needed to ensure these things do not happen even when passing through major crisis situations. Train yourself regularly; start as soon as possible, especially so you know how to move and how to react in different kinds of situations that may come.

Above all, to know, to be able to control your way of Breathing in even critical moments, and to be able to breathe correctly and beneficial for you and for what you have to do. ONLY in this way, through previous training, you will be able to cope with those critical moments that may arise at some point in your life and be able to control the situation, especially your body. To be able to control our Breathing and its rhythm, as well your body's reactions that may occur automatically at a given moment.

Only through previous training will you be able to set in the body's subconscious certain beneficial habits and specific actions, so when you need them, you'll automatically know the most proper and helpful action steps to cope appropriately and successfully deal with crisis situations.

The Deep Breathing exercises and the energy practices mentioned above greatly help your body set itself into "Relaxation parameters." Into your body's inner "ZEN" state.

To be able to connect to your deeper inner states. States where your Breathing changes. And it becomes slower and more profound.

- As a result, in the body, this disconnects from the Sympathetic Nervous System and switches it to the functioning of the Para-Sympathetic Nervous System.

In a state of Stress, Breathing becomes "short" and fast ("panting," "heavy").

In states of (natural) body relaxation, Breathing becomes "light," slow, and deep.

The best clue your body gives you (easiest to notice) regarding Stress and the situation when your body goes into a state of Alert, "Fight or Flight," is **BREATHING**.
The Rhythm of Breathing, actually.
When your Breathing becomes fast, short, limited, and heavy ("panting"), this is the sign your body's telling you it has already begun to "mobilize its troops" - **in response to the perceived "STRESS state"** that appeared.
When you notice yourself starting to breathe fast, short, and heavy, it is a sign for you that your body has entered the state of "Internal Stress," of "Fight or Flight" mode. (That means you are OUT of the "Relaxed," "normal" state.).
No matter what you are doing in those moments. It can happen to you at any time. This is why you need to pay close ATTENTION to these SIGNS your body is showing you.

Through consistent practice of natural relaxation techniques and energizing activities, you will be able to have under control and at your disposal (any time) the "control buttons" for **Relaxation, Regeneration**, and especially those for your body **Healing**, whenever it will be necessary. (Of course, ONLY with the condition that you DO NOT let others do different chemical or genetic experiments on you, regardless of whether those are called: medical forums, "doctors," Pharmaceutical Industry, WHO... etc. Cause, under those specific circumstances, you may end up **NOT having anymore full control of your body**.
Especially, you will no longer have full access to its natural Self-Healing abilities).

Relaxation is the only way to remove Stress from your life and avoid its harmful health effects.
(You can find more details about this in one of my other books from this series, dedicated to Stress: "Stress - The Ignored Enemy").

As I said before, it is good to practice your exercises somewhere outdoors, in the middle of Nature. Not only for the benefit of Breathing a much Cleaner Air but especially for the benefit of working and practicing with more "Aligned" Energies. Energies of Nature that are undisturbed. Not as there are in the big cities.
Thus, in Nature, you receive the advantage of "Aligned Energies," purer and more undisturbed, which are much more compatible and easier to assimilate by your energy system and body.

Breathing, and its huge importance on many levels, has been one of the best-kept "secrets" throughout the ages. Why? Because it relates directly to the energetic aspects of Human Beings. Also, it is one of the main "ingredients" necessary for activating "para" or "super" human Potential. Including those "extra-sensory" qualities and abilities. Thus, for some time, those in charge of the planetary leadership have NO interest in humans becoming "super-gifted" or "super-powered." Because this way could be a risk for those in charge, that people could become independent and thus out of their control, therefore end up being no longer controlled and manipulated.
And this does not suit at all with the plans of those in charge on this planet.

Many aspects and situations in life emphasize the very great importance of Breath. Even if we are taking into consideration purely only the physical aspects and performance. For example, in the case of athletes (especially performance ones), military training (especially elite troops), and dancers (singers as well), there is a strong emphasis set on awareness and training of Breathing and its rhythm.

Also, many spiritual practices emphasize how important **the process of Breathing** is. Especially to must have a **slow and Deep Breath**. This is not only for the proper functioning of the Physical Body but also for the Subtle Bodies, the Energetic fields, and the Aura. Also, Breathing is an essential aspect of the harmonious development and evolution of your Being on many different levels.

In the Toltec teachings, it is said:

"If your Breath is agitated, your mind becomes restless.
To quiet your mind, it is best to start by Controlling Your Breath.
An angry person's Breathing is rapid and shallow and is located in the chest and head.
A relaxed person's Breath, on the contrary, descends into the abdomen."

That's why, in situations where your inner state becomes more tense, more stressed, and more agitated, you can regulate it and control it through the rhythm of your Breathing. A calm, slow and deep Breathing can help you to center yourself within. And thus can change your "mood."

You can also improve many of your daily activities if you start doing them by changing the rhythm of your Breathing by being deeper and slower. An "abdominal breathing" especially. This way, by breathing differently, you will be able to enhance all what you are doing.

Including even the internal energy and especially the "sexual energy," for example, you'll be able to control it much better through correct Breathing - slow and deep. Most of all, this helps you to center yourself and to relax. (Aspects entirely neglected by the uninitiated but very important and necessary to have a fulfilling and quality sex life).

Many people do not know that sexual activity is set "by default" by its construction or creation to be performed in a state of Relaxation, calmness, and depth.

NOT in states of "stress," agitation, or "hurry," rush... "fast-food" type. These rushing types of doing things are totally opposite variants to a deep erotic communion in a real Couple Relationship.

More specific details regarding Couple Relationships can be found in one of my other upcoming books, part of this guidebooks series for women.

Internal Respiration - Mitochondria

Another important aspect of the body, but at the cellular level, is the "**Internal Breathing**." Explained simply, this is how the body's cells receive Oxygen-Energy and eliminate Toxic Waste, or "toxic energy." This process is done through some "little Energy Factories" called: the **Mitochondria**. "Energy Plants," which are at the same time also "Coordinators" at the cellular level. Which, it seems (scientifically speaking) they are

quite independent, having their own DNA, and even reproduce, multiply, and develop independently of the cellular activity of the organism in which they live.
A cell in the human body can have many such "Energy Plants" - Mitochondria. Reaching up to 2000 - into a liver cell, or even 5000!!! - into a Heart muscle cell.

Mitochondria at the cellular level are responsible for the production and management of the body's Cellular Level of Vital Energy. Also, Mitochondria are in charge of producing some essential substances for cellular activity and vitality, called: **Adenosine Triphosphate (ATP)**. These are directly proportional to the body's Vitality, Youth, or Aging.
In fact, according to "Science," it seems these Mitochondria are the main elements contributing to the maintenance of Youth or the Aging of the body (if, or when, these Mitochondria start to deteriorate or degenerate).
Also, based on "scientific theories," Mitochondria are considered to be the energy producers at the cellular level in the body.

The faster these Mitochondria degenerate and are destroyed, the quicker and prematurely the body ages.

The better the condition of the Mitochondria is maintained in the body, the longer its Vitality, Health, and Youth are maintained.

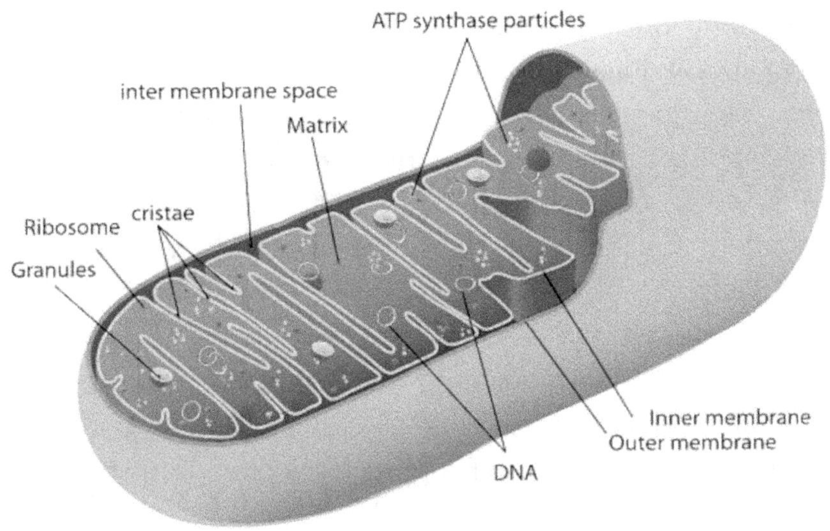

- Image: Mitochondria
(Photo Credit: Mariana Ruiz Villarreal (LadyofHats) - Public Domain - Wikipedia.com)

You can find more details about Mitochondria, their functioning, as well as about Cells in general on the website: www.cell.com

HOW might Mitochondria be helped to function better in the body?...

There are a few helpful elements that could be very useful for this:

1) - **Practice physical activities and Exercises**. Especially "Energetic" ones (like Tai-Chi, Qi-Gong, Yoga, etc.) help a lot, mainly if these are practiced outdoors, somewhere in Nature.

2) - **Fasting** (the absence of food eating) also helps a lot. It can be done one day a week, a few days once a month, or even once every few months.

It also helps to have your "Breakfast" later - after 11:00 (am) o'clock in the morning. Also, the evening meal - dinner, to have it no later than 18:00 - 19:00 (6-7 pm). So-called "intermittent fasting" has been promoted often lately, even among athletes.

For more details on fasting and how it can be done as correctly as possible (including understanding the processes that occur in the body in these situations), the book "The Miracle of Fasting" by Paul Bragg is highly recommended.

3) - **Sunlight**: it is recommended to spend at least 20-30 minutes in the Sun daily. But not to stay in the Sun very long when the Sun is very hot (11:00 am - 5:00 pm), during the summer time in hotter areas. (When the temperature outside exceeds 30°C / or 86°F)

Sunlight produces beneficial "PhotoSynthesis" at the cellular level in the body. This also helps the proper functioning of Mitochondria.

This process is also related to the so-called phenomenon that occurs in the water in contact with the Sunlight, called **"the 4th phase of water aggregation" - "Liquid Crystalline Water" or "Exclusion Zone" ("EZ water") - fourth phase water.**

The Crystalline phase is structuring water into some specific form.

More details on these aspects can be found in the materials at these following links:

https://www.nature.com/articles/s41598-019-44097-3.pdf

https://www.sciencedirect.com/science/article/pii/S0091302218300062

https://blog.mymetabolicmeals.com/longevity-secrets-taking-care-of-your-mitochondria/

Dr. Gerald H. Pollack - The 4th phase of water aggregation
(The Fourth Phase of Water)
https://youtu.be/p9UC0chfXcg

Including the above mentioned aspects, bathing in Sea (Ocean) water and exposure to Sunlight has a double advantage.

Thanks to these aspects and advantages brought to the body, it also explains the well-being that appears after going "to the Beach" or "to the Sea."

Of course, with the condition to not stay there too long if the sunlight is powerful. NOT during periods of 'hot sun' or 'burning sun.' In that case, various problems start to occur due to too much exposure to strong sunlight: sunstroke and skin problems, even reaching "Skin Cancer" for some people.

4) - **Exposure to cold or heat for short periods**. A few minutes of snow bathing, cold showers in the summer, and standing in the cold for short periods also help produce new Mitochondria.
So does sitting in a sauna (15-20 min) at high temperatures also help.

5) - Quality **Sleep** (see the following chapter in this book: "The SLEEP - Troubles, Problems in the Bedroom,
or Regeneration and Healing?...")

6) - **Magnesium** - which is best absorbed transdermally (through the skin), is an essential element in producing Adenosine Triphosphate (ATP - the scientific name given to the energy produced in the body by Mitochondria).

Thermal baths containing Magnesium and baths into the Sea, Ocean, or salt waters effectively absorb Magnesium into the body. It can also be helpful to massage some body parts with Magnesium Oil from time to time, mainly to the joints. Magnesium Oil also helps the cartilage and the body's joints.

7) - **Diet**: it also helps to eat a diet with as few Carbohydrates as possible and as many Good Fats as possible. These **Good Fats** are contained in Olives, Avocados, various types of Walnuts, Almonds, Cashews, Pistachios, Susan Seeds, Pumpkin Seeds, Flax Seeds, Hemp Seeds, Pine Seeds, Hazelnuts, etc. They also can be found in Pure Vegetable Oils ("Extra Virgin"), cold pressed, and made from those foods listed above Olive Oil, Avocado Oil, Walnut Oil, Almond Oil, Hemp Oil, Coconut Oil...etc.).

Harmful daily habits

Fluoride and a **"Fresh, Nice-Smelling Breath."**

Regarding the subject of Breathing, we can highlight the "Fake Information" about it: those for a "Fresh and nice-smelling Breath."
It concerns those products that are part of the "Dental Hygiene" range, where it is "recommended," in a very aggressive way, by the medical industry, the use of Fluoride, especially in Toothpastes, but also in "Mouthwashes" (those "Breath freshening solutions").

However, what is not specified (**AT ALL**) in their "recommendations" are also the **Toxic Adverse Effects of those Fluorides** on the human body. It mainly affects the Pineal Gland, one of the body's most essential glands.

Those Chemicals (Fluorides) help a lot but **ONLY help the Pharmaceutical and Medical Industries**. Fluorides are valuable "ingredients" for these Pharmaceutical-Medical industries because, in time, these particular "ingredients" bring them a lot of CUSTOMERS... automatically a lot of money too ($$$). This is due to the Toxic Effects those Chemical elements - Fluorides are bringing to the human body. Fluorides are affecting people's health on many levels. With major implications in affecting the Pineal Gland, one of the main endocrine glands in the human body. The Pineal Gland is said to be the "Gateway" or one of the "main bridges of connection and communication" between the physical body and the invisible, higher Spiritual Planes.

Thus, it seems that through the frequent use of Fluoride and its derivatives, it comes to the unpleasant "performance" of gradually calcifying this vital component of the physical body - the Pineal Gland. Thus, with the "help" of Fluorides, this main endocrine gland ends up not being able to perform its functions except partially. In this way, limiting the functions and parameters of this major endocrine gland a lot, this aspect also influences other processes and organs in the body, which are considerably limited or disrupted.

Thus, introducing Fluoride into people's daily "diet" became a "gold mine" for the Pharmaceutical-Medical Industry.

Fluoride, among other things, "helps" the body a lot for:

- Weakening (lowering) the Immune System (and when the Fluoride ends up somehow being combined with Mercury, the Immune System collapses!!!);
- Pineal Gland to calcify;
- The body, and especially the skin, to age faster because it mainly attacks Collagen Fibers. (These Collagen Fibers are the ones that give elasticity and mobility to the skin, bones, muscles, and ligaments);
- To slow down brain function, to make humans more docile, and easier to manipulate and control. Thus leading them into having a "**retarding**" behavior effect!!!...
- "Helps" tissues degenerate faster... Among the effects: brittle bones, wrinkled skin, hair loss;
- Fluoride also interferes with the production of red blood cells (Erythrocytes). When red blood cells are low, the body is forced to "supercharge" to produce the Oxygen necessary to feed the cells. **Anemia** is one of the results when there are not enough 'workers' (Red Blood Cells) to get the Oxygen needed for cell function. Thus, the body can no longer work at full capacity. But instead, with reduced "staff" (workers) - reduced capacity.
Effects as a result: fatigue, dizziness, breathing difficulties, shortness of breath, changes in heart rate, etc. may occur.

So, stay aware...

SMOKING habits

Another harmful habit against the body, **which affects mostly the Lungs, the Nervous System, the Brain, and especially the Oxygenation of the body**, is SMOKING.

"Each year, **one in five deaths is caused by a smoking-related disease. Deaths caused by Smoking-related diseases have a higher proportion than deaths caused by alcohol consumption, car accidents, suicides, AIDS, murders, and drug use together!!!"**

Smoking affects, in the first place, the proper **Oxygenation** of the body. Oxygenation is one of the PRIMORDIAL aspects of the body for its correct functioning and for maintaining a "potent" and active Immune System for maintaining good well-being of the body too.
Good Oxygenation of the body helps maintain a good state of Health and maintain the Youth of the body as long as possible.

You can document yourself and find many articles and information on the Internet about the Harmful Effects of Smoking.

For example, on these sites at the links below, you can find more information on the harmful aspects of smoking to the body:
https://www.cancer.org/cancer/cancer-causes/tobacco-and-cancer/health-risks-of-smoking-tobacco.html

https://www.lung.org/our-initiatives/tobacco/reports-resources/sotc/by-the-numbers/10-health-effects-caused-by-smoking.html

(It is worth pointing out that most of these harmful effects of smoking appear mainly due to modern cigarettes. In addition to the harmful health effects of tobacco (which is no longer genuine tobacco either), those cigarettes also contain many other chemical elements harmful to the body.)

More than **four thousand chemicals** (!!!) from cigarette smoke are active chemicals that cause catastrophic changes in the human body.

- The most harmful substances in cigarette smoke are tar, carbon monoxide, nitrogen oxide, hydrogen cyanide, heavy metals, ammonia, and radioactive compounds.

There are **43 cancer-causing chemicals in one cigarette**!!... The Nicotine contained in cigarettes is toxic and lethal in high doses.
When smokers take their "dose of smoke," they inhale thousands of other chemicals along with Nicotine!!...
Many of these components are chemically active and produce negative changes in the human body.

Dangerous chemicals contained in cigarettes:

- **Tars** - chemicals resulting from cigarette smoke: nitrogen oxides, carbon dioxide, and carbon monoxide. Tar is brown and has an unpleasant taste, stains teeth, nails, and lung tissue.

Tar contains benzopyrene, a highly carcinogenic hydrocarbon!!!

- **Carbon monoxide**: is an odorless gas that is fatal in large doses because **it takes the place of oxygen in the blood**.
A smoker's heart has to work harder to oxygenate the brain, heart, muscles, and other vital organs.

- **Nitrogen oxides**: animal experiments have shown that nitrogen oxides damage the lungs.
Nitrogen oxides are thought to be particular chemicals in tobacco that cause lung disease and emphysema.

- **Hydrogen cyanide**: the lungs have some pores (cilia) that help to 'clean' the lungs by removing harmful substances that get there.
Hydrogen cyanide inhibits the cleansing process of the lungs, meaning that the poisonous substances getting there from cigarette smoke remain there in the lungs.

- **Ammonia**: is a very strong chemical found in cleaning products. It is also used to preserve human organs at the morgue. It is also harmful to the lungs.

- **Heavy metals**: cigarette smoke contains dangerous metals, including heavy metals such as arsenic, cadmium, and lead. Many of these metals are **carcinogenic**.

- **Radioactive compounds**: cigarette smoke contains **radioactive compounds that are carcinogenic.**
How smoking affects the respiratory system:
- Irritates the trachea and larynx;

- Reduces lungs function and causes respiratory failure due to lung swelling and limitation of lung capacity;
- Causes excessive mucus inside the lungs;
- The inability of the lungs to clean and remove poisonous substances results in irritation of the lungs.

The effects of smoking on the circulatory system:
- Increased blood pressure and heart rate;
- Constriction of blood vessels, as a result, lowers the body temperature;
- Less oxygenated blood in the body;
- Agglutinating blood, which is prone to clotting;
- Damage to arterial lines, contributing to atherosclerosis (fatty deposits on arterial walls);
- Increased risk of heart attack due to blockages in blood circulation.

The effects of smoking on the immune system:
- The immune system no longer works well;
- Smokers are more exposed to infections;
- The body's healing process takes longer.

The effects of smoking on the muscular and skeletal system:
- Reduction of blood circulation in the extremities (fingers and toes);
- Muscle tension;
- Reduction of bone mass.

Other effects of smoking on the body:
- Irritation and inflammation of the stomach and intestines;

- Increased risk of gastrointestinal bleeding;
- Reduction of tactile and gustatory senses;
- The appearance of premature wrinkles;
- Increased risk of blindness and hair loss;
- Gingivitis.

Effects of smoking on men:
- Reducing the level of sexual hormones;
- Impotence caused by reduced blood circulation in the groin area;
- Increasing the risk of Cancer of the reproductive system, including penile Cancer.

Effects of smoking on women:
- Reduction of fertility;
- Decrease in sexual appetite;
- Reducing the level of female hormones;
- Absence of menstruation or irregular menstrual cycle;
- Increased risk of cancers of the reproductive system, including cervical and breast Cancer.

Effects of smoking on fetuses:
- Increased risk of miscarriage, spontaneous abortion, premature birth, or stillbirth;
- High risk of developing problems with attention deficit and hyperactivity;
- A smoking father can affect the fetus even if the mother is not a smoker; she is exposed to passive smoking;
Suppose the baby's mother also smokes during the child's first year. In that case, the child is at risk of ear infections, respiratory diseases such as asthma, sudden death

syndrome, and Cancer - like Chronic Lymphocytic Leukemia (CLL).

Diseases caused by long-term smoking

A heavy smoker is at high risk of developing fatal diseases, including:
- **All types of Cancer**, such as lung, mouth, nose, throat, pancreatic, leukemia, kidney, penile, cervical, bladder, and colon cancers;
- **Lung diseases** such as chronic bronchitis, chronic lung disease, and emphysema;
- **Coronary artery disease**, **heart disease, and heart attacks;**
- **Ulcer of the digestive system**;
- **Osteoporosis;**
- **Poor peripheral circulation, which can lead to amputations.**

Also, **under no circumstances is smoking allowed during Pregnancy!!**

Very HARMFUL, smoking during Pregnancy can lead to the following situations:
- **Premature birth, complications at birth, and stillbirth**;
- **Babies with low birth weight. Children with low birth weight have a higher risk of developing some diseases in childhood or adulthood and even death;**
- **Children suffering from sudden death syndrome;**
- **Children with reduced lung function.**
It is also imperative to consider and pay attention to 'Secondhand Smoking' too.

Passive smoking also has very harmful consequences for those **who regularly inhale cigarette smoke** from others.
It can cause in "passive smokers" the appearance of Cancer, predispositions to Cerebral Attacks, and Heart Attacks.

More details on these harmful aspects can be found on these websites and articles:

https://www.cancer.org/cancer/cancer-causes/tobacco-and-cancer/secondhand-smoke.html

Cigarette Smoking And It's Ill Effects
https://www.swapnamithra.com/2015/01/cigarette-smoking-and-its-ill-effects.html

What You Need to Know About Stage 1 Lung Cancer – Very Effective Cancer Natural & Home Remedies.
https://cancernaturalremedy.org/1260/

Verma, M., Das, M., Aggarwal, R., & Goel, S. (2020). Trends and patterns of second-hand smoke exposure amongst the non-smokers in India-A secondary data analysis from the Global Adult Tobacco Survey (GATS) I & II. PLoS One, 15(6), e0233861.

https://www.cancerresearchuk.org/about-cancer/causes-of-cancer/smoking-and-cancer/whats-in-a-cigarette-0

https://www.verywellmind.com/tar-in-cigarettes-2824718

With all these **Harmful aspects of Smoking** in mind, you can make some **Conscious Choices** to help you with certain habits in your daily life. To (consciously) choose ONLY those that lead you towards a Healthy and Happy Life. And not to lead you toward future Problems and Suffering of all kinds.

It's up to you which Daily Habits you choose:

- To Oxygenate, Nourish, and Vitalize your body?...

- Or to jam it, sabotage it, and create all kinds of health problems?...

More details about a healthy lifestyle and learning better how to breathe correctly can have it into another book written by the same author I mentioned earlier - Paul Bragg, who, together with Patricia Bragg, wrote a book: "Super Power Breathing For Super Energy, High Health & Longevity."

Also, for possible examples of correct breathing exercises, you can search on YouTube (or the Internet):
"Wim Hof breathing tutorial by Wim Hof"

Also, helpful information for individual practices you can find on the Youtube channels listed below:
- **"Boho Beautiful Yoga"**
- **"Yoqi Yoga and Qigong"**
- **"Yoga with Adriene"**
- **"QiGong Meditation"**
- **"WudangBing"**
- **"Mimi Kuo-Deemer"**
- **"Food Matters"**

Different types of exercises and information, so you can choose according to what suits best for each of you.

Chapter 2

The SLEEP

Troubles, Problems in the Bedroom,

or Regeneration and Healing?...

- Do you know how important to your life and health the Sleep is?...
- How important do you think it is to have quality sleep?
- What problems do you think occur in your body if you don't sleep well or if you don't get enough sleep?
- Have you ever wondered: "What happens during Sleep?... WHAT happens in your body when you sleep or when you Dream?"...
- Do you know what would be the right size of the Bed you sleep in?
- Do you know what the room you sleep in should be like for you to benefit from Refreshing, Rejuvenating, and Restful Sleep?

An essential aspect of personal "Feng-Shui" or personal "Zen" about what we do daily is Sleep.
Sleep is the fastest and most effective natural method of Regenerating and Restoring the body and our Energy Fields too. For "recharging with Energy." A restoration of Vital Energy.

As I highlighted in another book of mine, the one about "Stress" ("Stress - the Ignored Enemy"), Sleep is the best method of recovery in the case of "Stress," as well.

Sleep can help the body to enter the inner state of RELAXATION quickly.
Thus, Sleep has a major role in maintaining (or restoring) a good state of Health.
Also, good Sleep helps you a lot with the activities you have to do daily.
Among other things, Sleep and Restfulness help to refresh the entire body's Nervous System. The Nervous System is quite overloaded, overwhelmed by the actual civilization's daily "Stress" and its busy and rushed rhythm.

Considering the significant benefits that Sleep offers us, it is essential to have Quality Sleep. Just as important as having a Healthy Diet, exercising regularly, as well as having a Healthy and beneficial Sex Life.

Sleep Deprivation (lack of), little sleep, or poor quality sleep has immediate negative consequences on the functions of the Brain, Hormones in the body, and physical activities. It can cause weight gain and the risk of various diseases in adults and children. It can also cause, over time: Heart problems, Strokes and Brain problems, Diabetes, Depression, and many others.
Lack of sleep also leads to an inability to face or solve the problems that arise in life. Can cause quite a retardation regarding dealing with the daily situations or issues that may occur.

Correct sleep = the ability to find solutions and quick solving and manage different life situations.

Regarding Sleep, certain aspects are very important in order to have a Restful, Relaxing, and above all, Regenerating sleep.
First of all, sleeping in a clean room is essential, both physically and especially energetically.

It is also very important with WHOM you are sleeping when you are sleeping together with someone.
Because, during the hours of sleeping together and "intimate closeness", many energy transfers occur between the people sleeping together. So it's good to be very careful/aware to WHAT you "get" ("pick up") without realizing it during sleep.

Sleep Cycles and Melatonin

Alpha Frequency

During Sleep, different Brain Cycles are happening. During these Cycles, the brain enters different wave frequencies. Just like they are in the case of the "awake state" (the Beta Frequency), only those waves are on a different frequency.
The human brain works like an electrical circuit, managing its own electricity. This activity, which can also be measured, works in cycles per second, or hertz, and manifests in different Frequency bands: Delta (0-4 Hz), Theta (4-7 Hz), Alpha (7-14 Hz) and Beta (above 14 Hz).

Compared to the Beta Frequency ('the "awake" state of daily activities), the Alpha Frequency is a slower, lower frequency.

It is usually associated with light sleep but allows conscious functioning in certain situations. Alpha Frequency is also found in Meditation states.

Among other things, the immediate benefits at the physical level of the Meditation state ("Alpha state") are:

 - It helps to reduce the consumption (the "loss") of Oxygen (O_2) from the body by more than 50%!!!... In this way, the body can benefit from a surplus of Oxygen;

 - Carbon Dioxide (CO_2) from the body gets eliminated up to 50% faster;

 - Oxygenation to the Brain increases up to 90%!!!

Delta Frequency

This frequency corresponds to **"Deep Sleep"** (or REM Sleep - the 5th phase of Sleep). This is the time when the body, through the Brain, also produces **Melatonin** at its maximum level.

To produce Melatonin (by the Pineal Gland) in the highest possible quantity, the room where you sleep must be **completely dark**.

The more light there is in the room, the harder it will be for the body to produce **Melatonin**, the **'Hormone of Youth.'**

Melatonin is released into the bloodstream and then transported to all the organs in the body.

Usually, the Brain starts producing Melatonin about 2 hours before its usual bedtime.

Taking into account this aspect, in order not to complicate and "dilute" **Melatonin's** access to the organs and throughout the body, **it is highly recommended to stop eating at least two hours before going to sleep.**

After the body starts producing Melatonin, this process takes about 12 hours. It increases during the night and decreases in the morning when daylight appears.

Melatonin helps the body's processes, such as Circadian rhythm (Awake - Sleep, and daily activities), Sleep, Reproduction, Inner states, proper functioning of organs, etc. It is also involved in the functioning of the body's Immune System, in regulating blood pressure, as well as in regulating and balancing the Cortisol Level in the body. It helps to counteract Stress in the body.

(You can learn more about Cortisol - "the Stress hormone", and its role in the body in another book of mine: "*Stress the Ignored Enemy*").

In case of stressful situations, in the body, it is produced a specific hormone called **Adrenaline**. This hormone is referred to as: "**the aging hormone.**"

During a short period of time, Adrenaline can help you overcome specific critical, "life and death" situations. But, overused, being used excessively over a long time, Adrenaline can have unpleasant or even damaging effects on the body. You can quickly notice this aspect at the people who are "living their lives to the fullest," who are going through all sorts of "adrenaline-filled" situations. Their bodies start to look much older than their age. Even about 10-15 years older. To most of them, their hair also turns white very early: around 30-35 years old.

That's why it's very important to balance the respective states of Stress when it appears or other stress-demanding or stress-related states/situations of the body.

For this, **Melatonin** produced naturally by the body, called "**The Youth Hormone,**" plays a vital role in the body's balance and also into balancing the stress hormones produced.

Melatonin is also naturally contained in (edible) **plants and herbal juices**.

On the other side, at the opposite pole, '**the Aging Hormone**' - **Adrenaline**, is also contained in **meat and dairy products**.

In cases where someone sits in brightly lit rooms before going to Sleep, it inhibits (delays) the body's ability to produce Melatonin and thus be able to prepare for Sleep.

Also, looking (staring into, watching) at the "Blue-Light" of electronic devices such as cell phones, laptops, tablets, computers, etc... produces the same effect of delaying or even stopping the producing of Delta waves by the Brain and thus entering into the sleep state... maybe at its best only on to the Alpha wave Frequency.

That is, as a result, to arrive during sleep to the impossibility of adequately producing **Melatonin - the "Hormone of Youth."** But Melatonin is an essential daily regulatory substance for the body for Balancing, Rest, Relaxation, and Regeneration.

For this reason, **people who frequently use such electronic devices within 2 hours before going to sleep, over time, start to look much more tired and aged. They also get other health problems quite quickly due to the body's lack of proper rest (and Non-Recovery) during Sleep.**

The "Blue Light" also tricks the body into that: *it is NOT (yet) the time for sleep (respectively "the night"), but rather it would still be the "daytime."* Because "Blue-Light" is tricking the body, the production of Melatonin in the body is stopped, or significantly reduced.

An article by Harvard University (US) also speaks about the higher price paid in our modern-day living for all the artificial light used daily, impacting everyone's health because these influence sleep habits as well.

When sleep suffers, the whole body gets imbalanced.

These can have a contribution into causing: cancer, diabetes, heart disease, and obesity.

Also, **some studies put in evidence the link between exposure to light at night (such as night shift work) and the occurrence of some types of cancer, diabetes, heart disease, and obesity.***

Even something minor, such as low light during the night time and during sleep, can interfere with the production of Melatonin.

Other studies have also shown that the more the person lacks natural Melatonin production and intake during the night, the more they create favorable conditions for Depression. And not just Depression but also other mental health problems as well. This is very important to remember and consider, especially in the case of young people who tend to sleep less during the night or, worse, to waste their nights without sleep.

*https://www.health.harvard.edu/staying-healthy/blue-light-has-a-dark-side
https://northwestoptical.com/blue-light-and-how-it-can-affect-you/
https://share.upmc.com/2020/10/sleep-affects-mood/

For this reason, if you wake up during the night to go to the bathroom (toilet), it is highly recommended not to turn on the lights too bright. It would be best to have some special switches for the room, hallway, and bathroom that can adjust the intensity of the light. This way, during the night, if you use the toilet (or before you go to sleep), you can dim the light in the bathroom to a low, minimal brightness.

If the brightness of the bathroom, or the room, is too bright when you wake up during the night, it takes you out of those deep Sleep frequencies (Theta or Delta). It can also inhibit the Melatonin production process.

For a restful and refreshing Sleep for the body, it is highly recommended **to stop using those electronic devices with "Blue Light" (Phones, Tablets, Laptops, Computers.... and also bright lamps or lights, etc.) at least 2-3 hours before going to sleep.**

Very helpful during sleep is also to have turned off the Wi-Fi Routers at night. These emit enough Radiation during their daytime working time so it is no longer needed to radiate your body unnecessarily and UN-BENEFICIAL, even at night.

Another source of Radiation you carry with you all the time is the mobile phone.
Related to the Radiation emitted by GSM phones, it is very important to consider your phone's **SAR** (Specific Absorption Rate) radiation level. SAR is the level of Radiation absorption by the human body, measured in Watts per kg body weight (or/kg human tissue) = Watts per kilogram (W/kg).
This SAR level is different from phone to phone. Depending of the producing company, model, etc. The level of SAR radiation should also be specified by mobile phone sellers (as well as the other parameters of the phones). But unfortunately, the SAR level, the radiation level of mobile phones are aspects and information that are kept hidden (in most cases).
- Why is that, if these are some critical aspects of each one's health?...

Radiation always affects your health, more or less, depending on its intensity.

The Radiation Level ("*SAR*") of your phones would be better to have values below the range of **0.79 W/kg AT THE MOST!!!**

Just in case you do NOT want your brain to "fry" (over time) and your hair to fall out... also together with many other health problems (especially those at the mental-psychic level, such as depression, anxiety, panic attacks, etc.). All these could be triggered even by using a phone with higher level of radiation emissions. Mostly if you talk for a long time (more than 10 minutes) on your mobile phone.
It is also imperative to be aware and take into consideration the GSM radiation level of mobile phones, especially for children use. Children's bodies are more vulnerable than adults'.

In the case of mobile phones, the lower the level of **SAR** radiation value, the better. Ideally, it should be **BELOW 0.50 w/kg**.

More recently, related to mobile network radiation, the development, and implementation of the **5G** mobile networks (and devices as well) has already begun. This leads to even more amplified levels of radiation emitted: by the **5G** mobile networks and even more radiation emitted by personal **5G** devices and phones.

Also, from a while, Wi-Fi Routers with much higher transmission power have recently started to be implemented and are being used more and more. In particular, the "Gigabit" routers. These are set (by default) to transmit simultaneously (at a maximum 100% emission power level) onto two different channels (at the same time): 2.4 GHz and 5 GHz. (You can recognize them quite easily by their thicker antennas). Of course, they affect the human body more and more.

When it comes to sleep, the main age groups that end up suffering a lot nowadays from various sleep disturbances are young people, teenagers in particular. Even children at younger ages, between 6-10 years.

That's because now, in our busy daily life, many parents, in order to give their children something to do, to keep them occupied, 'hook them up' fast with one of those modern electronic devices.

The child is quickly fascinated and "totally" captivated (absorbed) by those "virtual worlds" they enter via smartphone, tablet, laptop, or computer... Or even with TV games, such as PlayStation, X-Box, Wii, Nintendo, etc.

Many children, young people, and even adults spend much time in front of "blue-screen" screens, phones, computers, laptops...etc. Especially in the evening and just before bedtime too. Many young people often waste (lose) their nights unnecessarily instead of sleeping and resting. These wasted nights also demand paying the 'tribute' for that - but the 'payment' is coming then in the form of health problems. Bringing health problems into the lives of those wasting their precious time needed for sleep.

There is also even another category: young people who spend (waste) their nights in clubs, bars, etc. For them, in addition to the fact that Melatonin is no longer produced, the presence of Alcohol (or other 'strong essences') makes things even worse for their bodies.

The "**Delta Frequency**" of the functioning of the Brain is the frequency that helps the most in the body's healing process.
(Or better said, this is a "Higher Frequency" to which the whole body is tuned, aligned).

Those Brain Cycles (in which the Brain enters on the frequency of the DELTA WAVES - ranging from 0-4 Hertz - cycles per second) can be produced during each cycle of **90 minutes of continuous Deep Sleep**. Then every other 90 minutes, another Cycle begins.
However, if during the sleep process, at some point you wake up (when someone touches you, for example, or if you need to go to the toilet), that respective **Brain Sleep Cycle** you were into is interrupted.
The brain then has to start its deep sleep cycle from the beginning.
This can happen not only to couples who sleep together.
It should be kept in mind and considered as well this sleep aspect, even including the parents or relatives who sleep in the same bed with their children, as well as those animal lovers who sleep in bed together with their pets.

This aspect of Brain Sleeping Cycles, should also be taken into consideration by those who do not manage to have a suitable and beneficial place to sleep.
Thus, the brain, if you wake up (even for a few seconds), is forced to interrupt that Cycle of sleep is into. In this case, the Brain will have to restart its Cycle ("countdown") again from the beginning... To start again from "zero."
By nature, women need to sleep with one more sleep cycle than men. That is, at least by 60-90 minutes more than men. (Per 24-hour day cycle, of course).

For them to be able to rest and recover properly. And also for keep themselves young, beautiful, bright, healthy, and in the best shape as long as possible.

In situations where those full **Brain Cycles of 90 minutes** are not achieved during sleep, the person in question ends up waking up in the morning more tired than she/him was before going to sleep.

For this reason, it is much better (even in the case of couples) that, at least from time to time, each one sleeps separately in different beds.

In this way, each of them is able to have the best possible rest, and regeneration can be achieved. Including not being disturbed during sleep. Thus each is completing those sets of full 90-minute Brain Cycles. Very important for regeneration and rest.

For example, four complete 90-minute cycles = 6 hours of sleep.

- 5 complete 90-minute cycles equals 7 hours and 30 minutes. That's approximately the "8 hours of sleep" many doctors recommend.

It is important also, every night, to achieve at least **a minimum of 4 complete Brain Sleep Cycles**.

Separate sleeping from time to time for Couples is also beneficial in order NOT to end up at a given moment to sort of energetic "limitation" or "Polarization." (From an energetic point of view).

If the situations where couples sleep together are maintained for a long time, the energetic "polarization" occurs in the couple's aura, into their energetic fields, in their lives. Over time, because of this, that mutual "Attraction" between the two partners in a couple can diminish, or even disappear. The "Attraction" between couple partners is mainly produced by the "difference" in the Energetic Polarity between the two partners (Yin-Yang, Feminine-Masculine).

So, it is not just about "chemistry," as some wrongly believe. Mainly thing is **all about Energy**.

Of course, many people don't even have a clue about the Energy, so they can't have any idea what is really happening into the Energetic Fields between two partners. At the level of their subtle fields.

(*More information about these aspects of "Couple Relationships" details, you will be able to find it in one of my future books, specifically about "Couples Relationships"*).

So, to avoid that mutual couple's **energetic "Polarization,"** it is good that from time to time (at least), the two Couple Partners sleep separately, each one in their own bed. So that they can optimally replenish and restore their own Energy during sleep. Restored energy, from which both partners can benefit.

The energetic "Polarization" in the Couples' energy field is one of the main causes (especially in older "couples") that could lead, over time, to the "routine," "lack of desire," or lack of attraction between the couple partners. This is also a result of the lack of personal (inner) "Practice" and "Inner Self-Work" for personal development and inner evolution.

Unfortunately, this way, most of the couples end up reaching that blazed attitude inside as if there is nothing "New," "Fresh" or "Alive" happening there anymore.

But these aspects don't happen (or happen very rarely) in the case of Couples where each partner is constantly Practicing "Inner Self-Work." Thus succeeding in living a more Quality, Conscious, and "Balanced" life.

"The Realm of the Dreams"

Also, during Sleep, something else happens, on a subtle, Energetic level, while the "Physical Vehicle" (the Body) is resting: those "Journeys in the Realm of Dreams," "Journeys of the Soul into the Astral Worlds."

These deep inner states of sleep cannot be properly accomplished if the body is periodically touched and respectively "awakened" during sleep time (even if only for a few seconds). This way, the optimal conditions for entering into the Deep Sleeping state (Delta Frequency) cannot be achieved anymore.

Unwittingly (without noticing it), usually during sleep, when someone touches you, you wake up from that "Deep Sleep" state ("getting out" of the Delta Frequency). So, you enter the state of wakefulness ("Beta Frequency") every time (or maybe only to the Theta or Alpha frequency level)... But either way, you get out of the "Delta Frequency" for the Deep Sleep state.

In that case, **Melatonin** can NO longer be produced because of your de-connection from the optimal frequency in which the production of Melatonin can be achieved.

Related to the "realm of dreams" and those "Astral Journeys" during sleep, someone can see the personal Level they're at by "scanning" themselves. E.g., to see what Level of development (and Spiritual evolution) some person is at. They can do that by monitoring their personal "Dreams" (or Nightmares) and observing WHAT (and HOW) they are "Dreaming." Mainly what they predominantly dream about.

Each Soul can ONLY "ascend" (access) to that "Spiritual" Energetic Level ("Realm") corresponding to their own level of Vibrations. Thus, depending on what someone is predominantly "Dreaming" about, this can show the "REAL" level the person is at her inner Soul's, Energetic, Vibrational level.

For example, those who predominantly dream "Nightmares," some "unpleasant dreams," or all kinds of "weird" dreams are those who keep themselves at the level of Low-Frequency Vibrations and Energies.

The "nightmares" and unpleasant dreams are the result of entering, during sleep, into the "Lower Levels" of the Astral Worlds. Or into those "*Hells*" realms (as they are also called).

On the opposite side, some dreams can transmit different "Messages." Messages that can Foretell or Communicate something important to you. Messages that come to help you with the Changes and Transformations you have to make in your life at some point.

Thus, if a nightmare occurs only sporadically, from time to time, rarely, it may be just a "Message" from the Universe telling you that "*you are on the wrong path*" in your life and you need a Change (or Changes) into your life. It might even tell you the "area" in your life where you need to make the respective Change (or Changes).

On the other hand, you can also receive various other "Messages" during Sleep from Higher Frequencies, sent to help you know HOW and in which areas to Change and Improve your life, like "Pre-Visions" (Previews).

These could include Ideas, even "Visions" (images), or landmarks for various projects, creativity, or something you could develop further in your life.

The Quality of Sleep

For a Restful and Reinvigorating Sleep, it is important to take certain aspects into account:

- The mattress you sleep on should NOT be soft because that way, you could end up having problems, back and joint pain;

- It is recommended the mattress you sleep on be an orthopedic mattress. Or even Super-Orthopedic - for those who can sleep on those;

- It is recommended that the mattress **should NOT contain metal** (to be without any metal elements) or **not to be a sponge mattress**, because over time these are generating dis-balances for the health;

Some other suggestions and recommendations for having quality sleep:

- **The bed and mattress should be comfortable and made of good quality**. Be aware of the fact that **you spend at least one-third of your living time there. It is also the place where you carry out two of the Core (main) Activities of your life**: **Sleep and also the Erotic Act (in the case of couples)**. So it's well worth your extra attention and involvement for that;

- Your bed should not be too narrow or too small because when you move during sleep, you risk waking up and thus interrupting those Sleep Cycles of the brain;

- The blanket, duvet, or comforter you cover yourself with should not be too heavy because you also risk waking up (and interrupting your sleep cycles) when you move (or rotate) in your sleep;

- The mattress, as mentioned before, should not be too soft;

- The mattress, including the bed you sleep on, is recommended to be replaced (changed) regularly, at least once every few years.
Maximum of 5-7 years - about after 2100 - 2700 nights spent there;

- The bedroom, or the room where you sleep, should have a 'clean' atmosphere and energy. Clean them frequently and regularly, both physically but especially energetically, in order not to risk any unpleasant "surprises" during sleep (meaning to avoid connecting yourself with bad or negative energies, or attracting parasites or nightmares);

- In the room where you sleep should not be too hot or too cold because, in these situations, you will not be able to sleep and rest properly;

- Regularly spend as much time as possible in nature and enjoy the rays and the light of the sun;

- Eliminate exposure to "Blue Light" at least 2 hours before going to sleep. DO NOT use during this time those electronic devices such as computers, smartphones, tablets, laptops, etc.

For those of you who really need to work late into the night in certain situations, it is highly recommended to install on laptops or computers software programs or apps that filter out "Blue Light," like "*F.Lux*" (you can download it from this site: https://justgetflux.com/). This is free.

Or another program is: "*Redshift*" (also free, but only available for Linux and Windows - http://jonls.dk/redshift/).

Or: "*Iris*" - https://iristech.co/ ($15 license).

Or use special glasses that filter the "Blue Light."

For Smartphones or tablets, there are various apps for that, like: "*Blue Light Filter*" or "*Night Shift -Bluelight Filter*";

- It is also recommended to avoid watching TV at least 2 hours before going to sleep at night. Also, avoid exposure to very bright light before going to sleep;

- Avoid eating anything at least 2 hours before going to sleep;

- Avoid drinking coffee or any drinks or beverages containing caffeine or other "energy boosting" substances in the evening (before going to sleep);

- Avoid drinking alcohol. Drinking alcohol at night can cause sleep and hormone imbalances. It disrupts the production of Melatonin during sleep at night. Alcohol is known to cause or exacerbate sleep problems, such as apnea, snoring, or sleep disturbances;

- Before going to bed, do relaxing activities. Listen to relaxing music, read a good book, take a relaxing bath, practice deep Breathing exercises, and practice Meditation. A good massage before going to sleep also helps a lot to de-stress and Relaxation;

- **NEVER** go to sleep if you are upset, angry, anxious, stressed, or tense!!!... In these cases, it is important to do different relaxing and enjoyable activities before sleep to help you change your inner state and mood **before going to sleep**. Listen to some good music, meditate or take a walk in nature, spend time in the company of good quality people, read something relaxing, take a relaxing shower or bath;

- Also, before going to bed, a bath, or a shower, is a **MUST** if you have had a 'busy,' demanding, or 'stressful' day, especially when you have had meetings with various people. Also, in case you have encountered during the day some **situations or people with a "heavy load" or negative toxic energies.**
If you do not take a shower, bath, or "Cleanse" after such encounters, you will not be able to rest well, and you will have a "restless sleep." You even risk dreaming all kinds of "weird" and "strange things." These are only the results of some Low (Bad) Energy Frequencies - "Negative Energies" you have encountered earlier. Also, in the morning, in this case, you will wake up feeling "tired" and quite "weird";

- Including a simple foot bath, 20-30 minutes in warm water with sea salt or rock salt (possibly with a few herbs or drops of essential oils in the water) can help you relax and release tension and accumulated negative energies;

- Walking barefoot, at least for a few minutes, into the grass or the sand helps a lot for "grounding" ("earthing") - to eliminate accumulated tensions and toxins. To get rid of the energetic toxins in particular and the "electrostatic charges" - especially for those who work a lot on computers or laptops (especially to the metallic ones).

Walking barefoot directly on the ground in Nature helps you to restore personal energetic balance and align it with the Energies of the Planet. Very important for a good tone and a good state of Health;

- It is also important to keep in mind that women need at least 60-90 minutes more sleep than men every day. And it is very important that women's sleep also includes **at least 1 hour before midnight;**

Sleep and the "Medical - Pharma Industry"

Unfortunately, the pharmaceutical industry is primarily concerned with growing its market and sales, profiting massively ($$$) from people's health problems instead of teaching people how to have a Healthy Lifestyle. More and more, nowadays. Health problems are induced more or less by the various lifestyle factors corresponding to the current civilization and "modern" times.

Among other things, e.g., the medical industry comes on the market with some products ("drugs") which are claimed to supplement the Hormones that your body naturally produces by itself. Usually, the natural hormones are produced in the body under the right conditions, of course.

Regarding the Sleep area and its derivatives, "Melatonin" (hormonal supplement) is also made available and "recommended" by the "Medical Industry" among others (This is in addition to the well-known and much over-marketed "sleeping pills").

Commercial Melatonin on the market is made mainly in 2 variants:

- Synthetic - made artificially, chemically (from what?!?);

- Another variant, supposedly a more "natural" version, made from hormones extracted from various parts of animals?!?... In particular, from the pineal gland of those animals...

(Of course, in general, not many details are given about the origin of the component ingredients of the various "medicines," "preparations," or "treatments" recommended to people. The secret about the ingredients is very well kept, under the pretext of the so-called reason of: "manufacturing secret").

What do you think?... **What kind of adverse Effects (and what Risks) could those artificial treatments have on you and your Health, especially in the long term?**... What kind of possible negative side effects?... Not only on the physical level but even on the mental, psychological, emotional, and energetic ones...

Please note and take into consideration that **it is NOT recommended to take external Melatonin supplements.**

- Just as **it is NOT good to take any other external "hormonal supplements."**

Because, as with other hormonal supplements, such as estrogen, anabolic steroids, or birth control pills, if you take them "**even once,**" you can end up **lose control over your body!!!** Because this way, you can block the "Receptors" that connect the Endocrine Glands with the whole body. This way, the person **becomes a prisoner in his own body.**

Considering that Endocrine Glands from the body are actually "Alchemical Transmutation" tools that do the conversion between the Energy Centers (Chakras) and the Physical Body, interfering with them has far-reaching and damaging consequences on many levels.

"The Energy Centers ("Chakras") are channels of conversion between own personal Energy System and the surrounding Energies - Planetary and Universal.

Just as is with **Morphine** - which, even if it is used "just once," -> thus **DEFINITELY blocks**!!! the body's ability to Restore and Self-Healing.

Taking hormones from outside body sources creates a dependence on external aids or treatments for the human body.

The administration of sleeping pills is also harmful to the body.

Into the Sleeping process, the body needs **to "enter" Naturally**, by itself, into the state of Relaxation, Rest, and Regeneration.

(And NOT by forcing it trying to do that).

Usually, the body needs to have its "shut down," during sleep time. Naturally. By itself. Not artificially.

Also, in this way, the body is inactivating its "Sympathetic" Nervous System, the one responsible for working into "Stress" situations and extremely dynamic activities. Meantime, also it is necessary to be activated and put in function the other

Nervous System: the **"Para-Sympathetic."** The one responsible for **Relaxation, Rest, Recovery, and Self-Healing.**

But this CANNOT be done by inducing an artificial state of "falling asleep." This is NOT the way to achieve **Relaxation, Rest, and Regeneration states for the body.**

By inducing artificial methods of "falling asleep," **the body CANNOT enter any more into the right internal STATE that helps it Recover and Regenerate.**

Artificial methods could only lead to a pseudo "sleep." And not to get the qualities and benefits Sleep brings into the body normally and naturally.

The best way to do is to ensure optimal conditions so your body can **naturally enter the state of Relaxation and Rest**. By itself. This way, you can know for sure that the other Nervous System, "Sympathetic" - the one responsible for "Stress" states "goes out of service" - so it becomes inactive. That means the other Nervous System ("Sympathetic" one), will NOT stay connected or active anymore, even during the night.

The administration of Sleeping Pills brings many other harmful effects to the body. These are coming in addition to the lack of the body's ability to connect to its inner states of relaxation, rest, recovery, and regeneration.

In addition to the predisposition for an **increased risk of Cancer, the development of Addictions and Behavioral Disorders,** in the case of taking sleeping pills, other possible problems may also occur (depending on the person), such as:
- **Burning or itching sensations in the hands, arms, feet, and soles;**

- **Appetite disorders;**
- **Constipation;**
- **Diarrhea;**
- **Balance disorders and dizziness;**
- **Shallow and fast breathing - dangerous aspect for people suffering from asthma or lung diseases;**
- **Dry mouth and throat;**
- **Bloating and flatulence;**
- **Headaches;**
- **Gastric hyperacidity;**
- **Stomach pain;**
- **The appearance of uncontrolled tremors in the hands or some regions of the body;**
- **Generalized weakness in the whole body;**
- **"Strange" dreams - predisposition to nightmares;**

Unfortunately, the so-called "modern medicine" does NOT come with a correct and appropriate Education to teach people how to have a Healthy and Free lifestyle. And how to avoid living a destructive ("junky") lifestyle.

Instead, all kinds of "products" (fake products) are promoted and sold on the market, including so-called "foods" that, over time, destroy both health and people's lives too. Not being anymore "Actual Food" but something that only resembles food ("Food Like"). This happens even regarding certain "drinks" as well.

Then, from the "medical" and "pharmaceutical" point of view, all kinds of "recommendations" quickly appear for the health problems that arose afterward: so-called "treatments." Which, for the most part, do nothing more but hide the "signals" (symptoms, or "pains") that the body highlights at certain times as inside problems. "Signals" highlight that "something is not right" there and something needs to change in that wrong lifestyle.

The "recommended medical treatments" then trigger other problems (perhaps even much more severe) or other various "adverse side effects." After that, different "treatments" are "recommended,"... and so on. A whole "weak chain"... But those who are suffering, more and more are the Patients ("Clients"), the people... NOT the Pharmaceutical Industry. The Pharmaceutical Industry is growing more and more, taking full advantage ($$$) of people's health problems.

By the way, it is good to be careful about some misleading tactics, used to confuse people. They use specific key "names" on their product labels where the term: "Natural" sometimes appears. Very often, this name refers (medically speaking) ONLY to a distinction between the product made in a laboratory = "synthetic," chemically, or being used as ingredients, some components originated from "Nature" = often from an animal (in most cases, dead, of course).

An example regarding these aspects was the one from the 1990s in the USA when it was a "trend" (Medical trend) about an "Estrogen" supplement ("Natural"!?!), which was recommended/prescribed to women massively: "Premarin." It was the number one "drug" prescribed at that time by the "medical industry." It was labeled as: "of Natural origin" (i.e., derived "from Nature"). It was produced from the urine of pregnant mares!!!... The product was a combination of several "Estrogens," but from Horses!?!... The product was highly recommended and prescribed as a "treatment" for women then on a vast scale.

But over time, the product ("Premarin") was found to be linked to cancers, strokes, heart problems, and heart attacks.

You can read more details about these aspects in the article in the link below:

https://www.idealmedicalcare.org/the-shocking-ingredient-in-natural-medicine/

Many "great discoveries" of Science and various theories have been based over time on the discoveries of some "scientists" or "specialists," predominantly focused exclusively on the Logical-Rational side of their brains. They have absolutely NO Direct Perception, or any Abilities, of the Subtle, Energetic Fields (Worlds and Realms). The Subtle Realms and Dimensions about what most of the said "scientists" have no idea there is anything beyond the visible, Physical spectrum.

Unfortunately, for the majority of "educated" people, **Direct Perceptions, Intuitive Abilities** are lost since school time. In schools children are taught and led towards docility and obedience to the specific "realities" promoted by the Main Worldly Control System. But above all the children are guided towards the predominant use ONLY of the Logical-Rational side of their Brains. At the same time, unfortunately, the very "official educational system" is inhibiting children's **Intuitive capacities and abilities**. Skills that are lost over time by not being used anymore. They become inactive.

However, the Subtle/Energetic/Esoteric Worlds and Dimensions have recently begun to be highlighted more and more by the "scientific world" as well, especially through Quantum Physics.

(You can study more about these aspects, e.g., in Michael Talbot's book "The Holographic Universe").

Also, many of the so-called "recent discoveries" of Science, for example, have been known and used by Traditional Chinese Medicine and Esoteric Schools for hundreds or even thousands of years.

In the "Scientific world," many "scientists" have been "stuck" in their Logical-Rational mind thinking (very LIMITED concerning the HOLISTIC Perceptions and Functions of the Human Brain and Mind). Not knowing how to find, e.g., the "scientific answers" to some simple questions about some exciting aspects of Nature.

Some of these kinds of questions were highlighted, for example, by Dr. Patricia Bragg as well, in one of her books about the "Transmutation" and "Alchemy of Nature":

"How do you explain that plant foods contain minerals that plants had no way of extracting from the soil where they grew?"

"How does a cow manage to produce milk that contains far more minerals than the grass it was fed on?"...

"Where does the hen get the minerals she needs to produce the shell of her eggs since they are not found in her diet?"...

"How does the horsetail plant (*Equisetum hyemale*) thicken and strengthen nails, even though it does not provide calcium?"

"How can organic magnesium increase the amount of iron in the blood since it contains no iron?"

"How is it possible for a dried plum to contain more minerals than a fresh one?...

Indeed, how?"

And so on...

THE BED

- Do you have health problems?... Change your bed!
- Do you have problems in your relationship as a couple?... Change your Bed!

Returning to the "Sleep" area, the place where you sleep, the bedroom, and especially the Bed, do you realize that this is the place where you spend more than a third (over 35% - 40%) of your lifetime?!?...
Moreover, 2 of the most important activities of an adult's life are happening there: Sleeping (Sleep) and Erotic-Sexual Activity.

Even more, there it is also the main place for your Refresh, "Recharge," Regeneration, as well as Healing your body.
This means that **the Bed is one of the Most Important Places (respectively objects) in your life**.
Considering these aspects of major importance in your life, do you think it is worth paying more attention to the place where you sleep every day?...
How many people are aware of this important aspect of their lives?...

Many people ask:
- "*What would be the proper size of the bed we sleep in*"?...
How big (or small) should be the bed we sleep in for to have a Comfortable, Restful, and Regenerating Sleep?...

First of all, there is no bed that could be "too big" for this.

But there is a risk of having **a bed that is too small**—even much too small, many times.

So how can you test/measure and figure out if **the BED you sleep in is somehow too small or is the proper one**?...

In the past, since ancient times, inspired by Nature and their Intuition, people knew how to make the proper sleeping place.

A very simple method, "*Darr-Kama*," can help you measure and figure out quite easily what would be the right minimum size suitable for each of you to have a Restful, Reinvigorating, and Regenerative sleep.

And this method can be applied for the ones who sleep alone in bed and also for those who sleep together with someone else, as well.

The proper **length of the bed** should be at least **20 cm longer than your height.**

(This way there, you should have available at least about 10 cm above your head and an extra 10 cm at your leg area of the bed).

For couples, the bed should be **at least 20 cm longer than the height of the tallest of the partners**.

However, the main 'problem'/issue in the world today regarding the size of the beds is mainly their **WIDTH**.
Usually, the Beds now in our modern days are **TOO SMALL** in width. **They are too narrow.**

(WHY do you think this is happening, as long this is NOT the most beneficial option for people?!?...
Why do they put first their commercial interests and not the people's interests in particular?...)

The Beds at the present time, in a proportion of about 70-80%, or even more, are **UNDER-SIZED** compared to how they should be "normally." For to be appropriate and beneficial for the PEOPLE.
It is important from now on that bed factories make a change and not make beds anymore as they are produced now, in most cases, just for Commercial interests, Real Estate interests...
Even the actual bed size names, those well-known types of: "King-Size" or "Queen-Size" beds, have commercial origins too. Those names appeared relatively recently, after the Second World War, also launched by the manufacturing factories.
But let's return to our bed measures and characteristics. So, how could be measured the right size of the Bed?... What

should be the minimum SUITABLE size of the Bed?... The width of the Bed especially.

It's very simple: using the "**Darr-Kama**" method of measuring the right size of the Bed.

As for the **Length** (long), I have already stated previously: it should be **at least 20 cm longer than the tallest person sleeping in that Bed**.

To measure the **minimum suitable Bed WIDTH**:

1) For those **who sleep alone** in bed, make the measurement (for the **minimum** bed size) in the following way, as in the following picture.

- To properly position yourself, lie down at the edge of the bed with one hand placed alongside your body, parallel to the edge of the bed. The other hand should be extended perpendicularly to the body, placed on the bed opposite the first hand, and stretched straight out at shoulder level. For example, if you are sitting at the edge of the bed facing up with the right side of your body close to the edge, place your right hand parallel to the bed's edge and close to your body. Meanwhile, your left hand should be extended to the opposite side, forming a 90-degree angle with your body and at shoulder level. It is important to ensure that the width of the bed is not less than the distance where your extended left hand reaches on the bed. This positioning is demonstrated in the previous picture.

2) In the case of **those who sleep together**
To determine the correct width size for a bed, follow the steps as it is shown in the following image.
Let's take, for example, the case of couples, where the woman sleeps on the left side of the bed and the man on the right side. (This is not a rule, the basic "rule" is **to feel as Comfortable as possible, as Restful and "Regenerated" as well):**
- To achieve proper positioning, both partners should sit close to each other relatively close to the center of the bed with one hand relaxed alongside their body and the other hand extended sideways at shoulder level, forming a 90-degree angle. The width of the bed should be at least the distance they reach together with their opposite hands outstretched, forming a 'T' shape. The minimum width of the bed should be wide enough to not be less than the up edges of the 'T' formed together by both partners.

Something as you can see in the previous image.

These are some simple reference points you can easily have when choosing your bed, for to have a Restful and Regenerating Sleep.

But the bigger the bed, the better.

As for the right room temperature to sleep in, there is no specific 'rule' for the most suitable temperature.
The base indicator is feeling **Comfortable** with the room temperature, which may differ from person to person, depending on the weather, season, location, etc.
On the other hand, as for the positioning of the bed, or how the room should be, including what else should be in that

room and what not, you can study more about it in the studies and information about the "Feng-Shui." This is the Art, the ancient "Science" of arranging houses, spaces, or the environment around you, to have the most beneficial Harmonization of Energies in respective areas. For a more beneficial Flow of Energy. An art originally developed in the Chinese culture but already widely spread and used in many other Asian countries, as well around the world.

You can also go directly to a (genuine) Feng-Shui consultant regarding these specific energy flow aspects.

But it is essential to find a GOOD, capable consultant with Active Extrasensory Abilities who **can directly perceive the Energies in a specific space**—NOT to be only a good "theoretician" about those subtle energies aspects. It requires someone who Directly Perceives and Feels the Energies. To be able to directly adapt the things and the components of the space in a particular way, depending on the place, adapted to the area in question and the people living or working there. Otherwise, it is better NOT to make "experiments" with amateurs or "theoreticians" because you will unnecessarily waste time, energy, and quite a lot of money.

Other recommendations for quality sleep

Some simple rules or points of view for a restful and regenerating Sleep:

- In the room you sleep in, it is good to carry out ONLY Relaxing activities. Including reading, listening to good relaxing music, practicing Meditation, etc.;

- The room where you sleep should NOT be used for work, job, or other stressful activities;

- If you have had a "busy," stressful, or tense day, it is highly recommended to take a shower or bath to clean your whole body, including your head, before going to sleep. It is essential to clean yourself if you had meetings or have been in the presence of many people during the day. Also, do that in case you have experienced unpleasant events or situations during the day or if you met stressful, negative, or toxic people.
Otherwise, you risk not being able to sleep well or not being able to rest. Or to attract "nightmares during your sleep."
(You can find more details about this in this book forward, in one of the the following chapters: "*Shower - Bath - External Cleaning and Energy Fields*")

Some "Feng-Shui criteria" to help you organize better your sleeping place and your sleep as well:

- It is beneficial in the room where you sleep NOT to have a WiFi router, active mobile phones (you can turn them off or

put them on "Airplane" mode), TV, and preferably no laptop or computer;
- It is recommended the Bedroom be without Mirrors, or other surfaces that "reflect" (like "mirrors"), such as TV screens, Monitors, etc.;

- Under the bed, you should not have all sorts of things stored underneath. Especially NOT those with various "heavy loads" - energetic, emotional, etc... or even worse: some with toxic, negative energies!!

- It is best if the bed is as "ventilated" as possible underneath so the air can circulate freely.
Another model of the bed type could be is the one with a compact bed structure down to the floor. That kind of model without that free 'airy' space under the bed. Without that distance between the bed itself and the floor.

As for storage under the bed (if, maybe), to keep there only "light" simple things, like bed sheets, pillowcases, quilts, etc. Only CLEAN ones. No other stuff. Possibly maybe pajamas, etc.;

- Metal beds are not recommended because they cause disturbances and imbalances at the level of aura and energy fields;

- The bed should not have any "heavy" corners or other "dangerous" elements in its structure.
Don't give yourself unnecessary Stress by having this kind of "dangerous" type of beds, where bumping into them could give you possible injuries or harm you.

Those "modern" ("fancy") or "trendy" beds that have all sorts of unnecessary and inappropriate "accessories" at the bottom, which can bump, hit and hurt your legs, are **not recommended**.

What do you think would be the "Meaning" for someone to invent and build such beds?!?... For bringing problems and unnecessary Stress?...

Such Beds are Contraindicated ("Forbidden") if you want to live a Harmonious and Happy life.

However, most of the current beds don't even meet the criteria of a **Suitable Size** anyway. Being too SMALL (narrow). Probably just like the life vision of those who designed and created them in this way.

Or perhaps, someone may want people to feel permanent (at some level) like "in the military," or... like in a "hospital bed"?!?....

The Sleeping Wear

As far as clothing is concerned, during sleep, the ideal would be to sleep without any clothing on to allow the skin and the body to "breathe" through all pores as well as possible. Also, allow the Energy to flow freely.

But, as I told you before, the essential criteria is you to feel **COMFORTABLE**. So, it's up to YOU to choose the most suitable clothing for your sleep.

Depending on the situation, you must figure out and adapt to what suits YOU best. If you sleep dressed, your pajamas, the clothes you sleep in, must be loose and comfortable. **NOT to be tight on the body.**

Because otherwise, it would block both your skin from being able to breathe and also your energy from being able to flow freely. Also, if the clothes are too tight on the body, they can block the digestive process during sleep.

Health problems caused by lack of sleep

In the case of lack of sleep, poor quality sleep, or deficient sleep, various problems can arise, highlighted in the picture below.

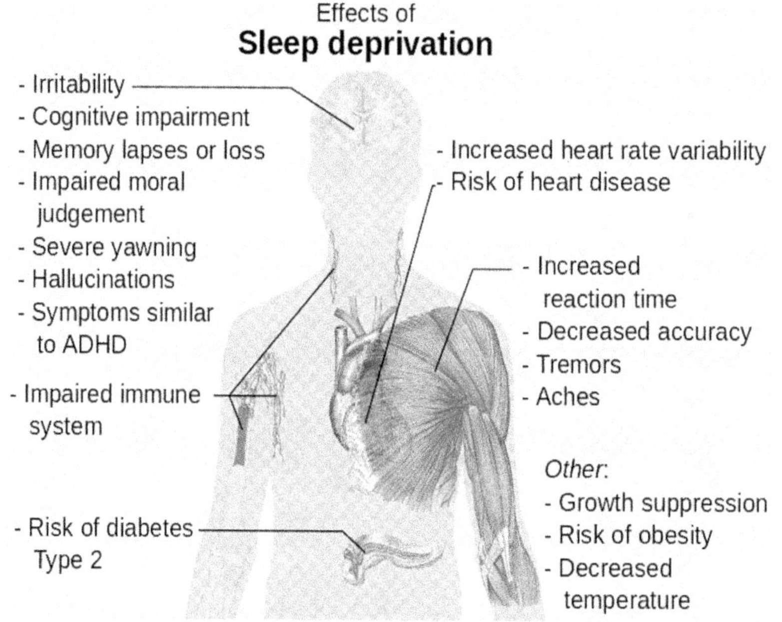

Photo credit: Wikipedia - Mikael Häggström

- **Irritability, nervousness;**
- **Memory loss or "lapses";**
- **Cognitive disorders;**
- **Immune system damage;**
- **Symptoms similar to ADHD;**
- **Hallucinations;**
- **Severe yawning;**
- **Impairment of judgment;**
- **Increased risk of type 2 diabetes;**

- **Increased heart rate variability;**
- **Increased risk for heart disease;**
- **Increased reaction times;**
- **Decreased accuracy;**
- **Tremors;**
- **Pains;**

Other: growth arrest, risk of obesity, low body temperature.

Also, another important aspect to consider is that: lack of sleep means also lack of natural Melatonin production (by "wasting the nights", i.e. not sleeping at night). This leads over time to psychological-mental disorders such as: **Depression, Anxiety...**

People who get less than 6 hours of sleep on a frequent basis, will have **more with 200%!!! an increased risk of having cardiovascular disease, or heart attack** during their lifetime.

(Acording to American Journal of Respiratory and Critical Care Medicine).

Also, as I mentioned before, Sleep is also the body's best way to balance the level of Stress in your life. The Sleep is also the best way for your body to "clean" itself inside and to remove the amount of Cortisol and Adrenaline from the brain and from the whole body. These 2 hormones are the main "Stress Hormones" the body produces as a response to certain situations you face in your life.

Thus, sleep deprivation brings you also the lack of possibility to balance the Stress levels in the body.

Prolonged stress is very damaging to the body in many ways.

Among them, we mention only a few of the most important:

- **Decrease of the Immune System;**

- Affecting the Endocrine System;
- Destruction of nerve cells in the brain;
- Promotes the occurrence of: diabetes, heart problems, various types of cancer, digestive and auto-immune problems.
These are just some of the possible health problems generated by Stress in the body.

(You can find more details in another book of mine, specifically dedicated to this aspect: "Stress the Ignored Enemy").

Chapter 3

MEDITATION
And the "Fall from Heaven"

- What do you think there are the necessary conditions your body needs to enter into the state of Self-Healing?

- What does Meditation mean, and why do you think it is necessary in your life?

- Did you know that Meditation can help you improve your Health and Quality of Life?

- How many minutes per day/week do you work with your body to improve its Health, Vitality, and Youthfulness?...

Did you know that from many years, successful people from all over the world, including "Hollywood stars" or those from the American show-biz, have been constantly practicing Meditation in their lives?...

Successful people and celebrities such as: Tony Robbins, Oprah Winfrey, Paul McCartney, Madonna, Will Smith, Jenifer Lopez, Jessica Alba, Katy Perry, Clint Eastwood, Sheryl Crow, George Lucas, Michael Jordan, Deepak Chopra, etc. are just a few of those who constantly practice Meditation in their lives to improve their lifestyle.

For many people, the constant practice of Meditation has been one of their secrets to success in life.

Meditation is, in short, the main way we can achieve the Alignment and Harmonization of ourselves and our Energetic Fields with Planetary and Universal Energy.
Energies that can then help us improve our lives.

Meditation is one of those essential "tools" or methods for personal practice and working with ourselves. The more consistently and also daily (or even a few times a day), the better.

Meditation is one of the necessary and valuable daily practices (and "tools") for a quality, harmonious, and happy life.

To help us, first of all, to calm our mind, free ourselves from Stress, as well to balance our inner states, emotions, various energies, etc.

Meditation helps us "work" with ourselves at higher parameters, depending on what we need to experience into our lives.

Among other things, at the inner basic level, **Meditation helps you to eliminate Stress from the body. It stimulates the body's Parasympathetic Nervous System and Relaxes the body's Nervous System.**

The **Parasympathetic Nervous System (PSNS)** is the nervous system responsible in the body, among other things, for **Rest, Relaxation, Recovery, and Regeneration**. It helps to Relax the whole body, especially after you experience stressful situations or stressful times.

This is the "key" and the way how the "Healing Frequency" of the body is produced. By switching (shifting) inside body parameters into the state of Inner Relaxation.

Meditation is also a way to help you make the switch inside your body, shifting from the Sympathetic Nervous System ("**SNS**"- the one for Action and response to emergencies and Stress -> **YANG** frequency) to the other Nervous System: the Parasympathetic Nervous System ("**PSNS**" - the one responsible for "Relaxation": Rest, Digestion, Healing - **YIN** frequency).

Meditation is also a way and a "tool" for "Purification of Mind" and "Purification of Consciousness." It helps you to reach the **inner state of Awareness**.

During **Meditation**, the **Pituitary Gland** is stimulated to produce many beneficial and pleasant substances for the body: **Oxytocin, Dopamine, Serotonin, Endorphins**, etc. These are most of the substances and hormones that can help your body get into the Relaxation state, have an inner State of **Well-being**, and also for the **Healing** process.

Meditation could also help you to awaken and activate Higher States of Consciousness. After the realization of the Spiritual Connection and Connection to the Divine Source is achieved.

Through Meditation, the Mind becomes Relaxed and Calm, and the Breath becomes balanced, slow, and deep.

Meditation helps to lower the level of Cortisol ("Stress Hormone") in the body and thereby helps to reduce Stress.

Meditation can also be a huge help to the Immune System.

Studies have shown that practicing Meditation helps to amplify in the body the substance called **Immunoglobulin A ("IgA")**, which is one of the main substances for defense against viruses and bacteria harmful to the body.

Moreover, **Meditation** doesn't cost you anything; it's **Free**. And best of all, it's simple to do, not complicated. It doesn't necessarily require specific "techniques," but rather, it depends on practice and constant training.

Meditation could also help you to develop and refine the process of Imagination, which is very important for developing your Creative skills.

Meditation could also help you Connect with your surroundings, environment, the Energies of Nature, the Planet, and the Universe. Meditation practice could give you the possibility to open a "channel" to the Subtle Worlds and other Energetic Dimensions.

Another beneficial side of Meditation is the inner "Scanning." A process and a "tool" that could help you observe more details regarding certain processes, interactions, and situations, both in your physical body and in your energetic, emotional, mental fields, etc.

In this way, you can train yourself to be able to detect (even in advance, long before) the various problems that could arise (or may occur), specific situations, or unpleasant (or bad, harmful) interactions that may affect you in time, sooner or later. Bad things could happen if you don't spot certain problems or situation in time, for to resolve them, to heal or transform them.

Even when certainly pains, unpleasant states or moods appear in your life, no matter if they are physical, emotional, mental, or energetically ones, you can use the "Inner Scanning" (Meditation) method ("tool") to detect and trace where they came from... or which is the REAL CAUSE that generated each of those problems.

Some of your problems in life could come somehow "picked up" from somewhere (or from someone), or even they maybe could have been "sent" towards you by someone, directly specific to your "address" (person, entity)...

(*You can find more details about the negative energies and how they can affect your health and your life in the next chapter of this book*).

Or Meditation can be used to "scan" and detect WHAT caused and generated that specific problem or unpleasant situation you are experiencing at a given moment. Mainly for you to be able this way to detect and SEE deeper.

This way, you could see and understand better what kind of "Messages" you receive inside of you, from your "Inner Voice," about what you have to "work on" to solve, to heal, or to transform to yourself.

This way, you can also have the opportunity to see and discover what are the Lessons you have to learn and be aware of from the unpleasant (and maybe painful) specific situation you passed through.

At some point, through constant practice, you will arrive to use the Meditation "tool" for something much more. Not only for "Fixing" and "Repairing" the Problems you have in your life but even more... Especially to generate, maintain, and keep your Inner State of Well-Being and have a life as harmonious as possible. (This will be possible only AFTER you solve your actual "Problems" from the present, but even more, especially those from the past).

Thus, you can generate a new inner state, to a higher level, on a different vibrational frequency. You can learn your life lessons from that higher level of Bliss and Prosperity. Also, from the Life Experiences you share together and co-create with those around you. And no longer be in those situations to learn your "Lessons" only from passing through Problems, Sufferings and Unpleasant or Painful Situations.

Reaching to a Higher Level of Vibration and Energy in your life, you will be able to move (switch) Your-Self from the stage of "**Karma**" to the one of "**Dharma**."

That's why it's much better to prevent than to end up searching to find solutions to "Fix" or to "Repair." (Sometimes, if you are lucky, you still can "fix" things... but many other times, what is "broken" cannot be repaired anymore).

The Importance of Meditation

To highlight how vital the Meditation process is, the Dalai Lama (the Tibetan spiritual leader) said:

"If every child up to the age of 8 had learned to Meditate, we could eliminate violence from the world within a single generation."

90

I don't think it's necessary to go into more detail here about Meditation's various methods or techniques, considering there are now many different options available on the Internet and on YouTube—a multitude of forms, techniques, and variants.

You can choose the ones you resonate with the best.

But essentially, during Meditation, the Mind must become as calm and Peaceful as possible, free from ephemeral, volatile thoughts. To achieve that, it requires to let the thoughts "pass"...

The paradox is that some of the so-called "thoughts" passing through your mind, which you think, believe (and assume) as being "yours," do not even belong to you... Instead, they are "picked up," "collected," or "induced" from "your environment" to you.

Thus, for all the "thoughts" not belonging to you consciously, it is essential to let them pass, let them go... and stop "hanging on" to them. To stop identifying yourself with them. Let them pass and just observe them passing by, like some clouds in a "clear" sky on a spring day.

Usually, a Meditation session should not exceed 20-30 minutes. Except that, in some "special" cases, where there is something specific needed to "work" with, in that situation it requires more time to be devoted to it.

Meditation can have numerous benefits to the human body and life in general, including:
- Reduces **stress and anxiety** - meditation can help reduce stress hormone levels and improve mood;
- Improves **concentration and memory** - meditation can help improve cognitive skills such as concentration and memory;
- Improves **physical health** - meditation can help reduce blood pressure, improve digestion, and slow down the aging process;
- Improves **interpersonal relationships** - meditation can help improve communication skills and develop empathy for others;
- Improves **sleep quality** - meditation can help improve sleep quality and reduce insomnia;
- Helps **spiritual development** - for some people, meditation can be a way to connect with their own spirituality and find their meaning in life.

Meditation can help a lot in the **Healing process**. It could help you adjust and align your frequencies and energies to the **Frequencies of Healing**.

But to achieve this, the person in question needs to BE in a particular inner State and generate emotional states of **Gratitude and Thankfulness** as well.

These are part of the **Holistic approach to the Healing process.** Otherwise, it is NOT possible to reach Healing. (Because in the case of health problems, if the real Cause of the problem is NOT solved, it then "moves" (passes to another area), triggering problems in another area).

Diseases, illnesses, and sufferings of all kinds are impregnated and imprinted on many levels in the body, especially into the people's personal "Fields": psychic, mental, emotional, energetic, etc.

Many people have been stuck in such a state of health problems for many years, with certain situations of Illnesses, so they have become accustomed (used to) to those unpleasant inner moods or states of suffering. Those health problems have become like second nature to some people. Those unpleasant states have already become a way of life for those people, integrated as part of their life. Thus, they became accustomed to living with those bad states of health and feelings, assimilating them into their lives as a "normality." Adopting them as "a reality" in their life. As "their own truth." Many people with problems can't even conceive of living without those Diseases, Illnesses, or Suffering of all kinds. Especially if people suffering from some diseases heard from their doctors: "You are not curable" or: "You will have to carry on those diseases and sufferings for the rest of your life." Thus, those ill people have "taken the respective health problems upon themselves" and carry them all their lives as "a cross to bear."

They don't even dare to ever think about anything different, about: "what if"...

The majority of the people don't even suspect that: **the more people suffer in their lives, the more they are "Energetic Donors" to all sorts of "Parasites" ("Demons," "Archons," etc.) from the Astral Planes (the "Invisible Worlds").**

(Yes, most people have no idea that there are other realms... invisible to the human eye. They only believe (are programmed by) in the so-called "scientific proofs").

Of course, those "Parasites" ("Demons") have no scruples and also no interest in people being Happy.

These "Demons"/"Parasites" are using all of their evil powers to influence and direct people toward all kinds of non-beneficial situations and circumstances so people end up **suffering** as much as possible. "Demons"/"Parasites" doing these through subtle energy manipulation, subliminal thoughts, and induced emotions.

Happiness = Stop Suffering = Stop "Donating" Energy to "Parasites." So, this does NOT suit at all those "Demons" ("Astral Parasites"). That's why they do everything possible to make people SUFFER, one way or another. As long and as much as possible.

More said:

- Suffering = Darkness;

- Happiness = Light.

Regarding all these, the idea of "Liberation," "Freedom," or "Exit from the Matrix" is mainly based on Freeing yourself from the bondage of suffering caused by those Astral Parasites from the Realms (Planes, Frequencies), invisible to the human eye. However, the paradox is that some animals, such as cats and even dogs, can perceive as well, even those Low Frequency (Bad, Negative) entities from the invisible planes.

About the principles and inner systems of Healing, the term "**remission**" itself - comes from: "**Remember Your Mission.**"

That "**Mission**" each of you has in this life, on this "Planet of Free Will" - Geea (Gaia). Except that most of you have gotten caught up in this maze of life, mind & psychic games and have forgotten **your own Mission**. Your **ROLE** to fulfill your Soul, the one for which you came in this life, on this Planet.

The moment a person comes **to FORGET** and "disengage" ("decouple," "disconnect") completely from their "Own Mission," their Soul begins to "disconnect" from the physical body. Thus, it begins **the process of "detachment" (disengagement)** to "leave from this Physical Dimension" - 3D.
This detachment ("disconnection," separation) then triggers all kinds of diseases and illnesses in the body, mainly those "incurable" ones. Also, these are usually fast "spreading" or happening fast, into the body, mostly as "Cancer." Those "Diseases" are, in fact, nothing more than the result of someone "Forgetting her/his Own's Mission" in this life. The result is the start of the "Process of Decoupling" and "Detachment" ("Uninstall") of their Soul and Spirit from their physical body.

Brain Waves

As mentioned in the previous chapter, the Brain Waves operate in four main frequencies.

1. "BETA"

The "Wake Up State," Awake, Conscious, or **"BETA Frequency**," is the frequency in which the Brain waves have a frequency of 14-28 Hertz (cycles per second).
This Beta Frequency is the state in which you are oriented to outer activities. It is the state in which you carry out your daily activities.

But an "over-setting/fixation" (switching on) of the Brain ONLY onto this BETA frequency leads to its **over-use (overwhelming, over-stress)**, which can lead to states of:
- **Stress;**
- **Depression;**
- **Anxiety;**
- **Panic attacks;**
- **Chronic Fatigue;**
- And many **other health problems** related to the **Nervous System, the exhaustion of the endocrine glands, and the body's vital energy.**

2. "ALPHA"

ALPHA frequency - is the frequency of entering into the "Meditation State," corresponding to frequencies between 7-14 Hertz (cycles per second). This frequency bridges the connection between the Conscious and the Subconscious, between the Beta and the Theta States of the Brain.

The Alpha state corresponds to the state of "**Inner Centering**," or "**Inner Alignment**," in which you Detach yourself and your attention from what is going on outside and focus Inside. It also corresponds to the state of Inner Calm and Relaxation.

Or, as it is also called in some esoteric schools: "The Second Attention."

Thus Meditation, the Alpha State of the brain, is the "Gateway" that allows you to enter and access the depths of your subconscious, the depths of your inner Being.

On the Frequency of 10 Hertz (cycles per second), the two Brain Hemispheres (Logical-Rational and Intuitive-Creative) begin to equalize (to balance), merge, and work as a whole, as one. **Alpha State is also the Inner State where one can access the Healing process of the Physical Body.**

Some Therapeutic Techniques, such as Reiki and Radiesthesia Techniques, for example, work mostly in the spectrum of this Alpha Frequency.

Also, those brainstorming and creativity groups work mainly on this Alpha Frequency as well.

3. "THETA"

THETA Frequency: is the Frequency between 4-7 Hertz (cycles per second).
It is the Frequency of direct access to your Subconscious and inner resources.
Also, "THETA" is the frequency for the so-called "Hypnotic State" or profound Relaxation. And Deep Meditation. It is also the frequency of the deep sleep state.

"Theta" is also the Frequency in which all your "Inner Programming" for how you function, comply, act, and manifest in this life" has been carried out since your childhood.

It seems that "THETA" is also the Frequency at which most children's brains are functioning. Generally, this happens up to 5-7 years old; children's brains predominantly function in the Theta and Alpha frequencies.

From the time of pregnancy until 2-3 years old, children are predominantly in the 'Delta frequency.' This is why the mother's inner states, emotions, and experiences during pregnancy and then during the breastfeeding period are crucial how they are because they are automatically transmitted ("absorbed") to the baby too. And the baby absorbs them fully.

This is why it is essential to be educated well during those first 7 years of life in childhood because this programs and structures the child's subconscious and

behavior as future adults. Those first 5-7 years of education have a powerful imprint and impact on the future life of every child.

That is why children's power of "absorption," openness, and receptivity in that period of childhood **is very high**.

The respective time of childhood is also called: "**the absorbing mind**" precisely for this reason.

This happens because of the "Settings" and the inner structure the children have in that period of their life. They correspond mainly to the Theta Frequencies of Deep Relaxation and Subconscious Programming.

Also, the Theta Frequency and the Delta Frequency correspond to the Frequencies of a more intense connection with the **UNI-Verse**.

Because of miseducation, generally, between the ages of 5-8 years, children's brains are "educated" ("domesticated," "indoctrinated") towards losing their inner abilities. Their direction forward means to enter little by little, ONLY onto **the Logical-Rational side** of their brain function. This is how the "educational" System settings begin to take the leading place in the children's lives. This type of "education" guides children to use their brains in the Alpha-Frequency state during their daily activities, except for when they are sleeping.

Between 8 and 12 years young, children already tend (being "educated"-" indoctrinated") to structure themselves and operate predominantly on the Beta Frequency of their brain. In the waking state, of course. That is only to Conform (to Obey) more and more to the "Peripheral Reality" (the "Shallow" or "Superficial" Reality) - of the 3D area. A "Reality" induced by the so-called: "education" (actually "the Programming" system, or "setting up") of the adults around them. Thus, children are "educated" to "comply and adapt to the world" around them... But which "world"?... The world of the "flock" or "herd"?... A "world" of mediocrity?... The world where to work and act as an enslaved person for others?... Is that what you want your children to align with?...

I sincerely hope NOT. And I hope that you will do your best to direct your children towards being able to keep and maintain, even after they grow up, their **inner Genius Frequency (and their Creativity, too)** - which, paradoxically, most children are born with.

4. "DELTA"

DELTA Frequency: the frequency of the Brain between 0-4 Hertz (cycles per second), corresponding to the deep sleep state (REM), the state of Dreaming.
It is also the state in which children's brains function predominantly from birth until the age of 2.

Delta frequency is where the body's main Self-Healing state is accessed.

But for this, it also requires, among other things, the person in question also consciously assist, help and support their own body in its Self-Healing processes. Or at least not to block, limit, or disturb the Self-Healing process of the body. It could be disturbed mostly through daily routines and habits: Food, Stress, Toxins of all kinds, Negative or Toxic Energies, etc.

In order to facilitate the healing process of the body, along with essential quality, restful, and regenerative sleep, there are other necessary aids. These include:

- **Healthy Nutrition** - first, by Eliminating Toxins that unnecessarily burden and over-loads the proper functioning of the body at its Optimal (Best) Parameters. So first, Detox. Second, as well bringing a supply of nutrients into the body;

- **Food supplements** containing those **"miraculous medicinal plants and herbs,"** especially those well-known in Asian traditions and Traditional Chinese Medicine, such as **Ling-Zhi (Reishi - Ganoderma Lucidum), Cordyceps Sinensis, Gingseng, Shiitake, Curcuma (Turmeric)**... and others;

- Practicing **Physical Exercises and Energetic Gymnastics**, such as **Qi-Gong, Yoga, Tai-Chi,** etc.;

- Doing daily **meditation** as well, at least 20-30 minutes. Also, at least 2-3 times/day during those periods when healing of the body is needed;

- **Amplifying and empowering the Connections with the Energies of Nature, Planetary, and Universal Energies through Meditation. Connect with the Divine Light as well;**

- **Deepening and Amplifying the Soul and Spiritual Connection.**

Meditation also helps to disconnect from the maze of the mind in everyday life stress. And from the "fast-forward" pace of the modern-day lifestyle. Constant Meditation helps regulate the daily Inner Rhythm. It helps re-centering and connecting the inner self with the Higher, Universal, Spiritual Realms.
A **constant practice** of at least **21 days** is required to set the body's internal system to a new frequency. Thus, you can set your body and your life in a new direction through daily, constant Meditation. The one you want, as far as this is **Appropriate and Beneficial** for you and your life. And for your **Evolution** as well.

There are many meditation techniques, and the most appropriate choice for you depends on your preference and the purpose for which the meditation is desired.

Some of the most popular meditation techniques would be:

- **Concentration meditation** - involves focusing on a single thought, thing, or aspect, such as breathing, a word or phrase, or an image, to raise awareness and achieve a state of peace and relaxation;
- **Breathing meditation** - involves focusing on breathing to reach a state of tranquility and relaxation;
- **Yoga meditation** - involves specific physical postures, controlled breathing, and focusing on an object or thought to elevate awareness and consciousness and achieve a state of peace and relaxation;
- **Zen meditation** - involves focusing on breathing, physical posture, and the present moment, without judging or analyzing thoughts, to achieve a state of mental stillness and clarity;
- **Mindfulness meditation** - involves focusing on the present moment and observing thoughts and emotions without judging them to reach a state of awareness and acceptance.

It is important to understand that each meditation technique can be beneficial in different ways, and choosing the most appropriate one depends on each one's individual needs and preferences.

Some of the multiple meditation options, you can find it on the internet.

You can find some on the Food Matters YouTube channel, (or by going to the link below):
https://youtu.be/gWAUVh7Okiw
- Also on the respective YouTube channel, you can find many other interesting and beneficial information.

Be As The Children Are

It is said in the ancient teachings:

"Be like the Children because only those like the Children will be able to inherit the Kingdom of Heaven."

It refers primarily to **the Innocence and Purity of children**. Moreover, it refers to the state of **Receptivity and Openness** the children have, set in such a way as to absorb as much information as possible and learn as much as possible from everything happening around them.

Also last but not least, it highlights the children's ability **to Be Present** in this **"Here and Now"** (an essential required feature of the "Spiritual Worlds") and to be detached from what is happening around them.

Aspects are possible due to children constantly being attuned to different (deeper) Fields and Frequencies of Manifestation and Expression: Alpha and Theta.

Different frequencies compared to the "fallen" states of the Adults (of the majority) around them.

Theta is also the "Frequency of Astral Travel" and the "Dreaming State" of spiritual masters and Light-workers. It is the Frequency of penetration into the Subtle Worlds.

Thanks to these aspects, **children can "SEE"** all sorts of things and Beings from the Subtle Dimensions around them without any problems. But adults (most of them) are already "anesthetized" and have limited their inner perceptions to use ONLY the 5 Physical Senses of the 3rd Dimension ("Beta Frequency"). So, of course, those adults don't believe children anymore about what they say. About what the kids can SEE from the subtle worlds and realms... *Kids with their sci-fi stories and nonsense*"... is how the adults think.

Additionally, in many situations, adults tend to reprimand children for what they perceive as imaginary or nonsensical, dismissing their experiences as mere "fantasies" or "silly things." For most adults, things that children see and perceive to a certain age can be found only in the pure "rich imagination of the child." Not even in "reality." That "reality" of the adults, of course. That is, the reality is limited only to the Beta level of functioning of their adult Brain (when they are not sleeping) and to the perception level of the five physical senses.

But the **Theta Frequency**, on the other hand, is also the "Healing Frequency" (of the holistic, energy healers), of intense Spiritual experiences, deep Connections with the Universe, past life regressions, of clear and very vivid Visualizations. This is why many children are able to access many of these aspects quite easily.

Aspects that most adults can no longer consciously access, being stuck/limited only in their Beta Frequency (because of a well-targeted "education," for that matter: an "education directed towards Logical-Rational and BETA Frequency").

That so-called "Fall from Heaven" can also be "translated" in a metaphorical way by "falling" down from the "Gamma, Delta, Theta Frequency" Levels... meaning, the falling from the "Higher Dimensions" (4D, 5D - of the Spiritual Realms) to the "Lower Spiritual Dimensions," the "3D" and the "Beta Frequency." From the "Depths"... towards the "Periphery" ("Shallow," "Superficial").

In simpler terms, these aspects refer to the distinction between an individual having access to their Capacities, Potentialities, Inner Abilities, and the State of Creativity - "Higher" evolutionary states and Spiritual development, (through the access to the Higher Levels of Evolution & Spirituality) - **versus NOT having access** (as: "falling" or getting stuck, "trapped" in the Physical, Material, 3D Level, or Realm).

These aspects and facts are also highlighted (in their own way) by the "current", "modern" science.

Through some studies done over time (in several countries, through a study coordinated even by NASA, before 2011), it has been discovered that, among other things, one of the significant valuable capabilities which we are born with as children on this Planet - **the Creativity**, this one it is present in children in a proportion of 98%!!!...

BUT... through the so-called process of "Education" and what comes afterward while growing up, "trained," and developing as adults, it comes around this percentage is drastically reduced by the age of 30 in the grow-up adult population. So, in the end, ONLY **2%**!!! of the remaining individuals possess active their **Creative Abilities**.

This could somehow be interpreted as well as a "fall from heaven," which occurs due to the process of "education" from childhood and then "schooling"... A process that is aimed at limiting children's Abilities and Inner Potential.

Children are mainly guided towards "training" and "education," focusing solely on their Logical-Rational abilities, neglecting the other side of their Cerebral Hemispheres. This results in them mainly relying on their five limited senses to perceive the world around them, leading them to operate only in the BETA Frequency state of their brains.

It seems as though this education is more suited for programming or training robots rather than humans. It appears to treat individuals as if they should only respond to specific commands, orders, instructions, rules, and norms.

And not as it would be expected for the education of some **Higher, Spiritual, Self-governing Beings, capable, among other things, about being able to create and be inventive.** And thus, to be able to "translate" (transpose, transmute) into the 3D Physical-Material Realm, the Universal Information, and the Energies that manifest and express themselves through those Beings.

This would mean an authentic Spirituality Authentic spirituality entails being the image and likeness of our **Creator.**

One of the unique abilities endowed to us by the **Creator is Creativity – the Capacity to Create.**

Question: HOW do individuals lose their innate Creative Ability that we are all born with?
WHAT causes that to be lost?...

Above all, WHO is interested in this tremendous inner Capacity and Potentiality ("Super-Power"), with each of us being born to be lost fast?... This is happening during the years of "Education" and "Schooling" (programming) to be "good citizens of Society (of "Consumption"), of the Social System"?...

Why is **the loss of these inner Abilities and Capacities also "coincidentally" related to the calcification of the Pineal Gland too?.... The so-called "Spiritually related Gland" of the body is the most important one. This essential gland of the human body, it seems, begins to calcify around 5,6,7 years old!?!... I mean, just about AFTER those first "7 years at home"?!?...**

Also, as another "coincidence," a vital Hormone of the body, "Melatonin" - the so-called "Hormone of Youth," is also related to the Pineal Gland...
In this case, the Pineal Gland starts to Calcify - already in childhood and to function at reduced parameters. But it still produces some **Melatonin** in the body, including other substances.
But, what would have been like and what would have happened IF this **"Hormone of Youth"** and other beneficial

substances had been FULLY, un-restricted produced in the human body?...
What if the Pineal Gland had functioned all life long at **its maximum parameters**?... Or at least at the parameters it had in earlier childhood?...

For the most part, the so-called "modern science" not only does nothing **to help people Wake Up (to Awake up) and Activate their LATENT ("dormant") Abilities and Capacities**. More than that, "the actual science" makes it so that **NO ONE** somehow awakes up but to remain in that "Sleeping" dormant state... A state where most people use only a maximum of 10% of their Inner Potentiality!!!... Predominantly using only the Logical-Rational hemisphere of their brain. That is just one extreme. And this is so they can be only **good Servants and well execute the orders and commands they receive**. But, for WHOM?... WHO is taking advantage of all these limitations and proper functional restrictions in human beings?
This is made especially for serving those who, for a very long time, skillfully run this Planet from the shadows in such a way that most people, well-controlled and manipulated, do not even realize it.

In this "educational" system, the other Brain Hemisphere - **the INTUITIVE - Sensitive ("Feminine" -Yin) side**, goes into a state of dormancy ("Sleep") due to its **non-use**.
But, especially for Women, this "education" and inner setting predominantly on the "Logical-Rational" hemisphere of the brain (that is, the predominant Male one) creates a great deficit in their lives. Because little by little, in this way, they

move away from their Feminine side and natural way of being, from their own **Feminine Potentiality and Intuition**.

What are your thoughts on the impact of computerized and virtualized education for children in today's world? Many kids have access to computers, tablets, and smartphones from a young age, as well as computer and TV games. What do you think this is leading to?
Where do all these lead to?... WHERE does this kind of current "education" of this modern time lead to?... What effects does it have on children's development (as future adults)? Or WHAT exactly does it inhibit?...
This is a possible "subject to reflect on" for you.

Regarding meditation, if it is accompanied by periods of "fasting" with no food, or where one only consumes liquid food or pure spring water, it can aid in creating a conscious connection with the subconscious.
"The Detox," the Elimination of Toxins from the body through "Fasting," ensures a clearing of the Mind and an improvement of the brain functions.
Also, periods of Fasting, then combined with Healthy Eating, Physical Exercise, and a constant practice of Meditation, for example, helps you get rid even of those problematic "Migraines." They simply disappear.
"Migraines are also Signs that your body is telling you that SOMETHING in your life is wrong and needs to be CHANGED.

Using these methods and "tools" of life, you could increasingly achieve a Healthy, Fulfilled, Happy and Harmonious life.

It is ONLY up to YOU and the choices you make—moment by moment, throughout your life.

Every Thought, Emotion, Feeling, Inner State, and Various Energies influence your Energetic Fields. They also influence, imprint, and structure your body (Physical Body) subconsciously, up to the level of DNA itself.

They can also structure, generate, and influence even the Future of your life from here on, implicitly the Experiences and Life Situations you will go through.

For this, it is essential to be aware and attentive to every word, thought, inner state, or energy you emit into the ether (into the Universe) into your environment because they shape your life and future.

Live your life Consciously, in the Divine Light, with Wisdom and Love!

https://www.health.harvard.edu/staying-healthy/what-meditation-can-do-for-your-mind-mood-and-health-

Chapter 4

The SHOWER - The BATH

The External Cleansing and the Energy Fields

- Have you ever wondered why do you feel so "over-loaded," drained, de-energized, or tired, especially after specific meetings or events?...

- How much do you know about the "Aura" and personal Energy Fields?

- How important do you think it is the cleaning of your Energy Fields?...

If it is also essential to clean your Energy Fields, how often do you do it?... And how do you do it?

- Did you know there is a way to "refresh" or cleanse your Energy Fields quickly?

As you probably already know, we are surrounded by Energy Fields. We find ourselves in an "ocean of energy" all the time. It surrounds us and is everywhere around us.

Even though these Energy Fields are not visible to the "naked eye" (through the limited five senses, "3D"), they have been able to be revealed with various more sophisticated devices by current Science.

Through Quantum Physics, these Energy Fields have been studied and called: "Morphogenetic Fields."

Scientific research highlights the same aspects: the existence of Energy Fields ("Universal") that manifest everywhere around us and even inside of us. **Everything IS Energy**.

The information about the Energy Fields all around us is one of the most important aspects of life here on this Planet. Including one of the best-kept secrets throughout the ages. Why is that?

If people were aware of these essential aspects of their lives, they would start asking more questions regarding this, about their lives, and particularly questions about what happens to them on this Planet.

These are uncomfortable questions, especially for those who have long held Planetary leadership and control for a very long time. Those who have grabbed and monopolized the planet's resources for a very long time. But mostly, the Human Resources. Specifically, **the Human Energy Resources.**

This is why these more profound and subtle facts and aspects of life are kept secret: NOT to be known by the vast majority of the masses. If these aspects and information were made public, it would strongly affect the Planetary Social System of Control itself. The Mass Control System was well developed and put in place by "some". The so-called "Matrix."

A System in which ONLY a small part of the people, less than 4%, own the majority of the Resources on this Planet?!?... WHY? How would the others be inferior?... Or, how the majority of people have done wrong, in one way or another, so they could not equally benefit from those Resources on this Planet?...

Many people still believe in illusions like: "my country," "my religion,"...etc. People have the false illusion that those resources or values from an area, country, religion, etc., somehow belong to them too. But this is a big illusion. Through mass hypnosis induced since childhood through education and school, and then through TV and media, the vast majority of the masses are directed in a well-targeted way toward **OBEDIENCE**. Thus, the "herd" does not even suspect that those resources and values of "their own country" belong to others, NOT to the majority, but only to a very small number of people. Often, paradoxically, that small amount of people owning those resources do NOT even belong to that specific country... or at least to the main religion of that country.

More recently, another kind of "control system" of imposition and changes "forced by circumstances" has been adopted. Launching out specific "problems" in the world, they can also come up after a while with some "saving solutions." (Something similar as it is in the case of "computer viruses." At some point, some specific type of computers can be "infected" with viruses, so then they can come up with so-called "anti-virus saving programs.")

But what people don't realize is that many people's personal freedoms slowly disappear in the time between those so-called "problems" and the appearance of the "saving" solutions. These are being reduced little by little, without even the majority of people realizing it.

We'll not go into detail here about those Energetic-Planetary aspects. Perhaps we will elaborate on these aspects in one of my future books.

We'll now focus on becoming more aware of personal, individual Energy Fields.

More importantly, by knowing how to do so, you can maintain these Fields at a level of manifestation suitable and beneficial for you and your life.

Cause Energy Fields are everywhere: around you, inside your home, workplace, vehicles, shops, cinemas, hospitals, other people's homes, etc. Especially inside and outside your body. In your so-called "Aura."

"The Aura" is the term that defines, in short, the totality of your Energetic Fields.

Energetic Fields that, whether you know about them or not, believe in them or not, implicitly they influence your life, directly or indirectly.

Having a significant influence on your health and your life in general.

That's why it is vital to be aware of them, to take them into account, and to do so in such a way as to ensure these energy fields are ONLY beneficially influencing your life.

Just as essential the hygiene and periodic cleaning of your physical body is, as well as your house, garden, workplace, the city where you live, etc., it is equally important, or perhaps even more important, to cleanse your **Energy Fields** periodically.

For thousands of years, in Asian traditions, these energetic aspects of life were taken seriously. Specialists in those areas knew how much these energies influence people's lives. So much so, for example, in China in the past, anyone who wanted to build a house first had to get the approval of a 'Feng-Shui' specialist from the emperor's court. "Feng-Shui" is a traditional Chinese science and art that has studied the aspects of energy fields and their influence on people's lives for thousands of years.

It has been well known since ancient times that: negative energy fields can cause health problems, financial problems, relationship problems, and all sorts of issues in life, and in some extreme cases, can even lead to death.

Taking these energy aspects seriously, Traditional Chinese Medicine, for example, studies and treats the patient **holistically, entirely, as a whole**. Considering (for treatments and the healing process) mainly the person's Energy Fields and Energy Meridians, their circulation, and proper functioning within the body.

As I said, energetic cleanliness is much more important than cleanliness on the physical level because the energetic aspects of your fields determine both your life, but especially your future. As well as influencing your health too.

It is almost the same as how you prepare, "arrange" yourself, and "get ready" for various activities, special occasions, or special meetings. For those occasions, you prepare, wash and get ready on the physical level for those situations or events. Equally important is to be aware of, make arrangements, and take action, even at **the energetic level**, for the various activities and situations in your life.

You need to take care of your personal energy fields and the energy fields of the space where you live or work too. Even more for the situations where you carry out more special activities or tasks.

Just as, for example, you can't eat anywhere or anyhow (at least that is what would be recommended), hygiene is important both in the place where the food is prepared and where it is eaten, and mainly for those who prepare the food. Equally important is also the **'energy hygiene.'** Both of the places and the people.

The negative energies of certain places or certain people can have a negative impact on your health and your life.

On the other hand, the presence of positive, beneficial people, as well as some places with more special energy, (a High Vibrational energy), can elevate and influence your life in a better way.

There may be negative energies in your life that come from certain people, places, or areas you regularly encounter. These energies can have a harmful impact on your life, causing a variety of problems.

Looking at things from an energetic perspective, specific aspects, and **points of view (POV)** can assist you in understanding the current situation you are in at a given moment. It is essential to pay attention to those "**signs**" that appear, mainly due to encounters and meetings with Negative, Toxic, or Parasitic people (or in various non-beneficial places).

Those negative effects/"signs," or bad feelings or emotions inside yourself (your inner mood), may appear immediately after such encounters or after a while. It is highly recommended to take note of these issues and take appropriate measures and action to avoid potential health problems.

Because, about this kind of energetic issue, the doctors you go to don't know what would be the cause of your problems and, therefore, will prescribe you some random drugs that will do you more harm than good.

In situations where you come across Negative, Toxic, or Parasitic energies, you may experience various types of problems, inner feelings or reactions, such as the ones (one or more) listed below:

- Strange feelings and sensations in your stomach or abdomen;
- Vomiting or vomiting sensations;
- States of nervousness or stress, appearing "out of the blue" without any real, well-founded reason;
- Feelings of anxiety, restlessness, anguish, or inside feelings such as: *"something is wrong,"* *"something is not right"*;
- Cold shivers, sensations (chills) on the spine;
- Sudden feelings of limpness, malaise, lack of energy, severe drowsiness, or even fainting;
- Sudden and repeated yawning (especially at some unusual times during the day);
- The appearance of fear or dread, like this, suddenly, all of a sudden;
- Feeling of strong pressure or pain in the head (especially in the forehead, temples, or cerebellum/occiput);
- The feeling of not being able to think or express yourself verbally coherently;
- Feeling or states of dizziness and mental confusion;
- Severe pain in the "head of the chest" or the neck or shoulder blade area. Also could include the feeling as if: "someone stuck a knife in your back";
- Another aspect more specific to women (but implicitly quite "dangerous" in many cases, considering the reason "behind" the respective sensations, as well as the subsequent non-beneficial consequences) **is the sudden "excitement," "arousal," at the sexual level, in the presence of certain men.**

Including certain sensations like "butterflies in the stomach"... Very often, these signals are simply warnings or alarm signals, that your body uses to grab your attention and indicate that "*something is wrong there.*"

These kind of specific "sensations" that suddenly appear to you around certain men ("males," "macho") are not just simple "arousal," "excitements," or "hormones that suddenly go crazy" (or "got out of control")... but these instead are the results of some **energetic attacks** directed towards you in certain moments or situations that you face at a given moment. Actually, you are dealing in those moments with an aggressor (or some) who **attacks you on a subtle level**, thus trying to penetrate and take control of your Energy Fields.

Those seemingly "innocent" games of "flirting" are actually attempts to explore, to "conquer" and take control of the person in question (woman or girl as well). From there, the next step into the "manipulation and control game" with that specific woman is only a matter of time... The true face of the "male" in question emerges (is revealed).

The reality is that: this "flirting thing" was far away (NEVER actually) from a so-called "love" or a possible "couple relationship" (as perhaps wrongly expected by the woman in question), but actually, it was only about a **Possession and Control** of the "male" in question, over that respective woman.

So, **be very careful** when you experience such inner states (moods), inside feelings, and situations listed above.

When one or more of the aspects mentioned above appear, they can be triggered by: **negative energies, parasites, "energy hooks" (or "hang-ups"), and non-beneficial or toxic energy connections**—some dangerous and harmful issues for you and your life.

That's why it is essential to be aware and careful (as **a woman or a girl**), WHAT KIND of people you meet, what kind of places you visit... and so on.

Be aware of that because some negative people or places can influence your life in a bad way.

Take note of the "Signs" specified above, and correlate them with the times when you notice that "**you feel sick**" or "being hurt." In this way, you can detect **the real CAUSE of the "Evil"** and eliminate it from your life.

Also, another very good reference point is to observe your Breathing regularly. **Your Breathing Rhythm**, to be more specific. When your breath becomes jerky, panting, and "short" (i.e., "Stressed"), your body draws your attention, signals, and alerts you that there: "something is going on" there. It is something that requires your focus and conscious attention to it.

In the event that you "get sick" due to energetic causes, without realizing what has happened to you, you then go "to the doctor" (I am referring here, especially to those from the "Western world"), you will end up in this way, without wanting to, becoming one of the "guinea pig" of the respective doctors. Because those "doctors," in the vast majority of cases, not only have no idea about **the Energetic aspects of your Being**, but worse, they start to make assumptions about what they think are the "causes" of your problems... But only on the physical level, of course. The respective "doctors" and the current "Medical-Pharmaceutical World" do not perceive more. (In fact, they are Directed since school time not to be able to perceive more. That is, NOT to sense or perceive as well from the Subtle Fields of Energy. NOT to see and understand on a Holistic Level). They end up being limited ONLY to the level of perception of the 5 Physical senses.

After that, then doctors start recommending "treatments" (to "treat" you), according to what they "guess" could be the "cause" from which you got sick!!! "Treatments," which, of course, are NOT beneficial to you since your problem was triggered by some negative aspects, attacks, and negative or toxic energies, at a subtle, **energetic level**.

HOW could anyone ever solve an energetic cause or problem, ONLY through treatments at the Physical level, especially with the allopathic, artificial "treatments" and "drugs" (that are **not compatible** with your body)?!?...

"Treatments" (allopathic) on a physical level come with various adverse side effects. They can bring additional problems into your life!!... Some Physico-Chemical problems, this time induced by the Medical-Pharmaceutical industry's cruel "incompetence" (bad intention?).

It is NOT just "incompetence," as it might seem at first glance, unfortunately... Rather, some much bigger interest is at stake. There are billions of $$$ that the Pharmaceutical-Medical Industry collects annually as a result of "recommendations and treatments" at the expense of (to the detriment of) people's health. Many deaths are recorded yearly due to this so-called medical "incompetence." In the USA, for example, according to official statistics, the so-called "misdiagnosis" of doctors is the third leading cause of death in the population. And this is true in other countries too. That says a lot about the medical world, especially about the link between doctors' incompetence and people's poor health. But this aspect, of course, brings even more $$$ money into the pockets and accounts of some of those directly involved in this Medical-

Pharmaceutical Industry. Unfortunately, the major interests are directed towards (huge) profit $$$, and NOT towards the people's health.

With all this in mind and the issues mentioned above, it is essential for you to be aware of and to practice working with yourself in your daily life, including **regular energetic cleansing**.

How can you do this? You can call a Feng-Shui specialist or a genuine therapist. But only those specialists who have results "in the field" and can mainly **perceive the subtle Energetic Fields directly.**

But the basic idea is to set, develop and evolve yourself to a certain level of Energy and Vibrational Frequencies, allowing you to do that periodic cleansing by yourself whenever needed.

How could you realize those **energetic cleanings** yourself from time to time?...

First of all, through your thoughts, in your mind, set as an intention, by inner centering, by **Relaxation, calm and inner peace.**

Through your **Breath and your Presence**.

Through **Connecting yourself, your inner self, your energy fields, to the Source, to the Energy Fields of the Universal Light.**

Through the so-called "**Raising of your inner Vibrations.**"

These practices can help you create protective fields for yourself and clean certain spaces, areas, etc.

You can also help yourself with **burning incense, sage, incense sticks**, etc., to cleanse the spaces and places where you carry out your activities. The important thing is that the incenses are hand-made, not industrial.

Certain **essential oils** can also help to cleanse negative energies and protect you and specific places and spaces. Be careful; avoid putting essential oils directly on your skin, as they can cause irritation or effectively 'burn' your skin. Mix them with olive oil, coconut oil, or other vegetable oil "base."

Also, the presence of **quartz crystals** in certain places of your house or where you carry out your daily activities helps to protect you energetically and cleanse those spaces. These crystals can help you on many levels, energetically, in your life. But it is very important to first 'cleanse' them energetically after you buy (get) them.

Also, it is necessary for those crystals, periodically, to be "cleaned" and "discharged" of the non-beneficial and negative energies they absorb from the environment in which they are.

- Unfortunately, there are also situations where the best solution for certain people, or a certain family, is to leave, to move away from that non-beneficial or negative place.

Some areas have very negative or even toxic influences on certain people or possible (specific) activities carried out in those places.

For example, non-beneficial places, or places with very strong negative energies, can influence an activity or a business and even lead to bankruptcy. Or they can negatively influence people's health, even to the extreme limit, leading to death.

In terms of cleaning the premises, just as the prayer of thanksgiving and gratitude is used before eating a meal, it is just as important to **energetically cleanse the premises and**

spaces before eating and especially before preparing the food.

The energy of that space directly influences the person(s) preparing the food. Their energy, emotions, attitude, and inner feelings are directly transmitted to their environment, to their surroundings, and to the food they prepare. Energies, emotions, and feelings are imprinted in the food and transmitted to those who eat it.

Considering these energetic aspects, a (healthy) food can also have the characteristic of being able to 'heal' those who eat it - through the beneficial contribution it can bring.

On the other hand, when the negative attitudes, harmful, negative, or toxic energies are not taken into account (when preparing food), there could be a risk of "sickening" those who eat such "toxic" prepared foods (from an energy point of view).

Just as it is important to energetically cleanse the spaces and the premises before preparing food or before eating a meal, it is equally important to cleanse other things or aspects of life energetically. Or before other similarly important life activities. Among these is **sleep**. It is very important to have as well the place where you sleep energetically clean.

Equally important, or even more important, **is to energetically clean the space and the respective place, before each erotic communion (the intimate, sexual act), in the case of couple partners.**

The Erotic Act, in essence, is a sacred act, which is why it is necessary to be treated and respected as such.

The Erotic Act can be a "springboard" (a "launching gate") to help you evolve and develop in a short time if you respect its sacredness... Or, on the contrary, it can "knock you down" to the ground easily and quickly, in the case you let negative energies and the primary ("animal") primitive instincts devour (consume) you from within.

In the moments of intimate connection between two partners, "some energy gates are opened"...

Depending on the energies of the two partners and the energies of the space where the erotic act takes place, through those "energy gates" or "portals" that open at a subtle level, different energies enter (penetrate) into the energy fields of those two partners. **Those energies coming are attracted by resonance, depending on the level of frequency and vibration (at the energy level) of the two couple partners.**

If the predominant energies of the two couple partners (Yin-Yang) are low-frequency ones, portals are opened, and low-frequency, "negative" energies are drawn (attracted) into the Auras (energetic fields) of those two partners.

On the other hand, if the predominant energies of the couple partners are high vibrational, then higher, Light energies are attracted. These can help the spiritual and soul evolution of both partners.

For this reason, in order to be able to attract beneficial energies during erotic communion (and not various "demons" or "parasites"), it is very important first to clean the space and place where the erotic act takes place.

Also, a very important aspect regarding the couple's relationship is **Choosing the Right Partner**.

- *More details on this aspect can be found in my next books.*

However, more detailed information about couple relationships and erotic communion between partners will be available in another book of this series of guidebooks, specifically dedicated to the aspects of couple relationships, with more particular, specific, and very useful information, especially for girls and women.

Another "tool" for energy cleansing, a personal one this time, is a practice commonly used by each of us. Or at least it should be.

It is one of the essential aspects of life, both for personal hygiene and for energetic cleansing: **"showering," bathing, physical cleaning**... That is, **washing the body**. Which necessarily includes washing your head and hair, as well.

A cleansing process that can help you eliminate unpleasant smells, accumulated dirt, impurities, and dead cells ("waste" and toxins), which form on the skin. The skin is the largest organ of the body.

But above all, the shower or bath can especially **help you cleanse your aura and your energy fields very quickly and effectively.**

It is the most accessible "method" of personal practice and cleansing that anyone can use.

It is even one of the most handy and convenient ways to relax and relieve stress accumulated during specific periods or over time.

This energetic bathing, washing, and cleansing would **ideally be done somewhere in Nature (as much as possible): preferably in a river, running water, or into the water of the Sea, the Ocean, or a lake with salt water, etc.**

Even some pools with thermal or mineral waters are very suitable for this, especially for their benefits to your body with the minerals these thermal waters contain.

If it is not possible to bathe, wash and clean in those different options within Nature, it is good as well to do it even in the "domestic" ("home") indoor options. That is, at home. They can also help a lot.

These baths can help you maintain a state of well-being and good health for your skin and the whole body. It helps to maintain good skin health - allowing it to perform its functions as well as possible and to have supple and beautiful skin.

What other 'ingredients' you use to wash yourself (meaning: shower gel, soap, or shampoo) is also very important apart from the water itself.

Water is better to be Chlorine-free, Fluoride-free and as little calcareous as possible, or none at all.

It would be ideal to use for washing yourself as "soap," something that contains as few chemical elements as possible.

In particular, it is very important to avoid using chemicals (contained in various "cosmetic" products) that are not too friendly to your body or skin. They dry and wrinkle your skin very much.

It is crucial to prioritize the washing and cleansing of your aura and energy fields, particularly after experiencing a stressful or demanding situation. This will help maintain your overall energy.

It is also good to take a bath or shower, especially **when you feel "overloaded" and "weighed down" by stress or bad and negative situations/emotions and energies you passed through.**

128

It is essential to do this personal "Cleaning,", especially after those situations where you have been in the presence (company) of many people at various events, such as concerts, meetings, presentations, seminars, and parties... including weddings, baptisms, weddings, birthdays, anniversaries, etc... as well as when you are traveling.

Above all, **especially and MANDATORY (!!!), it is important to clean yourself, to shower, to bathe after participating or being in more unpleasant (bad, or negative) environments or situations, those with some "strange" or low-frequency energies, such as funerals, cemeteries, hospitals, prisons...etc.**

It is also important to include cleaning yourself up after you have met on certain days sick, ill, toxic people or people with different problems.

After such situations, encounters, or meetings, it is MANDATORY to shower or to bathe as soon as possible afterward!!!... Including washing your head and hair as well.

This is an essential aspect, to shower, to bathe, especially for not to take in any low frequency/"negative"/"toxic" energies from those events, situations, people... and to not be influenced by that in your life afterward.

The faster you cleanse ("get rid") of those negative, NON-beneficial energies for you, the better.

Because most of the time, after such situations, most of the participants "pick up" (absorbing) all kinds of "**energy toxins**" and various "**energy parasites**." Low frequency and non-beneficial energies => "**negative energies**."

Then, after a while, **people can end up experiencing all sorts of unpleasant situations, conjunctures, and problems in their lives**. Those problems can be influenced (directly or indirectly), "triggered," and generated even by those "negative energies" picked up by participating in those respective events and encounters.

Negative results and consequences can appear immediately, or after a period, sooner or later, including various "health problems."

Many of the problems arising from the accumulation (burden, overloading) of negative, toxic energies may have "unknown causes" to current "medical science." Those problems could have subtle, energetic (Negative) causes that triggered them.

In such cases, medical science will not know what effective "protocols" or "treatments" to prescribe. Thus, as I said before, they will start to take a "guess," offering "at random" some possible "treatments," which, of course, will come together with their **specific Adverse Side Effects**.

Side effects that the same poor men and women will have to endure and then struggle to deal with. Thus, step by step, entering into a "vicious circle," which, if it is correlated with the more "powerful" - more dangerous and harmful "procedures" or "treatments," such as Chemotherapy or others, then the "accommodation" in the Cemetery is already "booked."

But all of these could be starting initially, perhaps only from some "Parasites" or some **"Negative Energies"** taken as a result of participation in specific "meetings" in some Negative, Low Frequency (energetically), Non-Beneficial, etc. environments.

130

Even more, as many of you probably already know, some people are so-called "**energy vampires**" or "**toxic people.**" It is highly advisable to s**tay away from this kind of people**, no matter WHO they are in your life. They are **HARMFUL** to you!!!... To you, to your health, to your life.

Keep this in mind: NO ONE is going to build you a statue because you, at some point, sacrificed your health, your life, and the Divine Energy manifested through you in this life... And so you wasted it uselessly and needlessly at the disposal of some Parasites.

On the contrary, YOU will be put, at some point, in the situation **to be "judged" and to "pay**," in one form or another, for the fact that **you "made fun" (or jokes) of your life and the Universal Energy invested in YOU**. That is, as a result, you wasted it.

People can absorb problems, negative energies, and toxic emotions at different gatherings or events. These issues can feel **personal and as if they belong to the individual**, even though they originated from someone else. They were not making the connection in any way with the "event," "meeting," "conjuncture," or "connection" previously had. But all these can be a significant contribution and "trigger" (through the accumulated "negative charge") for various problems, unpleasant situations, or various "health problems," which may appear after a while in the life of the person.

It is essential to consider and take into account these aspects, even if you may not (yet) believe or have yet to learn what **Energetic Fields** mean and represent. **These exist all around you**, inside you, in your (**Holistic**) System and your

Energetic Fields, as well as in your Environment and EVERYTHING surrounding you.

(Even though these Energetic Fields cannot be seen "with the naked eye" by the vast majority of people through the Physical, "3D" senses).

But for some time now, even the "Scientific World," through Quantum Physics, Epigenetics, and Energy Medicine, has increasingly begun to highlight these "**Morphogenetic Fields**" and take them into consideration. And even more, to make them "public." Somewhat. In various environments. That is available to those who want to know more.

Considering all the previously listed aspects, you should inform yourself about WHAT you are dealing with in the subtle, Energetic Fields. So that, afterward, not to suffer from the unpleasant Consequences - Results. These will not delay appearing in your life sooner or later if you don't consider them and don't take them into account.

Every deed, action, (including thought) of every person, including yours, represents a "Cause," which generates, in time, an "Effect." Sooner or later, depending on WHAT you have generated before the "Effect" (Result) appears in your life. This is the Universal, Energetic, Spiritual consequence of your own actions. Action-Reaction. Cause-Effect. It is one of the Universal Laws.

For more information regarding these aspects, I recommend you watch and study the following documentary films:

- **"Law of Resonance" ("Das Gesetz der Resonanz") - with Gregg Braden and Dr. Bruce Lipton;**
- **"Thrive" - parts 1 & 2;**

- **"Resonance - Beings of Frequency";**
- **"The Science of Miracles."**

Some useful books in the same area:
- **"The DNA Field and the Law of Resonance: Creating Reality through Conscious Thoughts" - Pierre Franckh;**
- **"The Divine Matrix" - Gregg Braden;**
Also, and many others...

Useful links for some more information:

Microwave frequency electromagnetic fields (EMFs) produce widespread neuropsychiatric effects including depression
https://pubmed.ncbi.nlm.nih.gov/26300312/

Wi-Fi is an important threat to human health
https://pubmed.ncbi.nlm.nih.gov/29573716/

https://www.iarc.who.int/wp-content/uploads/2018/07/pr208_E.pdf

https://explore.globalhealing.com/10-shocking-facts-health-dangers-wifi/

https://www.sciencedirect.com/science/article/pii/S0013935118300355

https://wellnessmama.com/health/wifi-safe/

https://heartmdinstitute.com/detox-toxins/wifi-dangers-what-you-cant-see-can-hurt-you/

https://www.cancer.org/cancer/risk-prevention/understanding-cancer-risk/known-and-probable-human-carcinogens.html

Conclusions

I hope the information you've read in this book has been helpful in addressing some important aspects of your life. By prioritizing your inner being and considering its needs, you can improve your life and gain greater control over it.

Breathing, Sleeping, and Meditation are three major aspects of your life. It is very important to be aware of them and take them into account to improve the quality of your life.

Breathing is one of the body's main ways of nourishing. And energy replenishment too.
Remember that it is important to breathe through your nose. This way, especially if the breathing pattern is slow and deep, the body relaxes.
When you breathe through your mouth, the body goes into alert mode. This makes the body tense up and start producing those 'stress hormones.'
Sleep is the quickest and most profound way to restore the body and heal.
Sleep is also the best way to remove stress from the body and to refresh and restore the brain.
For good refreshing sleep and for deeply restoring the brain and the body, it is necessary during the day to do physical exercises.
Meditation is one of the 'tools' to work with your inner-self, available to anyone, to go beyond the level of the conscious, rational mind and thus to go deeper within. To penetrate the

mysteries, the programming, and the operating systems, from the Subconscious and the Super-conscious. Therefore, be able to rewrite their programming for to experience a life full of fulfilling Experiences, which will help your evolution and development on many levels — a life as happy and harmonious as possible.

Without Meditation, crossing the "boundaries of the rational and conscious mind" is almost impossible. Thus, you will remain stuck within the limited framework of the "3D level of the logical-rational mind and the five physical senses".

Showering, Bathing, and Energy Cleansing are the "working tools" needed for both your "personal practice" and your couple's relationship life as well. These can help you release and eliminate the stress in your life, as well as help you eliminate negative or parasitic energies that may occur at some point.

Also, **Choosing THE RIGHT Couple Partner** for Yourself is an aspect that can elevate the life of both Couple Partners.

That's why it's very important to give this aspect the proper value and attention it deserves.

Otherwise, at the opposite pole, an inappropriate or toxic (parasitic) partner can knock you down and create you a life full of suffering and pain.

Remember that **Choosing Your RIGHT Couple Partner** is all about **YOUR inner RESONANCE**... And NOT about some "hunting," "chasing," or "searching."

But to attract someone who suits your Soul. For both of you. For both Couple Partners. For the **Development and Evolution together.**

You attract into your life NOT what you "want," but **What You Are, What You Emit, What You Resonate, What You Vibrate.**

What you are emitting is a specific Frequency of Energy of Vibration, which emits a certain specific Resonance.

That is why it is said:

"BE the change you want to BE in the world."

It is the same in the case of Choosing (Attracting) the Right Partner (for yourself) in your life.

In conclusion, it is good to keep in mind the following as a central reference point:

- When you are tired, feel strange, or start to feel some "bizarre," unpleasant feelings or bad inner states at some point, the most important and prioritary thing you have to do for yourself in those moments is to do **your Energetic Cleansing.**

Top priority!... Very, very important!

Do your Energy Cleansing for both of your personal energy through showering, bathing, and spiritual practices, and to the space, place where you are as well.

To ensure that negative energies do not impact your life in an adverse way, it is important to remove them from your aura and surroundings as soon as possible. This can help ensure a beneficial and positive impact on your life.

You need to consider all these and do the necessary energetic cleansing in time to avoid having different types of problems because of these.

In the spiritual, esoteric environments, one of the basic rules to have a harmonious life is:

- When your energies and vibration level get low, and all kinds of problems or unpleasant aspects begin to appear in your life, the most important priority is: **to raise your Vibration Level as quickly as possible.**

So, BEFORE you start thinking about what and how to do, or in what way to solve those problems or unpleasant situations that appear in your life, seriously consider, first of all, taking care of:
Raising your own Vibrations and your environment's Vibrations.

The great scientist Albert Einstein said: "*You cannot solve a problem from the same level as the problem itself is.*"

How could you "*Raise your Vibrations*"?... First of all, by getting out of the state of Stress and setting yourself more and more onto the inner state of **Relaxation**.
For this, it can be beneficial for you: a good quality Sleep, Meditation too, as well some practice of energetic exercises (in Nature, would be ideal), walking in Nature, etc.
For "raising your own Vibrations," eating as healthy and light as possible, fasting periodically (food breaks), including that "intermittent fasting" (quite trendy lately), can also help you. And there's more, also including the other aspects I've outlined throughout this book.
The following books of "The Feminine Ascension" series will cover even some other methods and practices for health and life improvement.

From somewhere "higher up," from "above," you can see and observe much better, the bigger picture... To know the best solution to solve the situations you face at a specific moment.

Problems and unpleasant situations in life often arise due to various negative energies, parasites, or energetic "hangings" ("burden," "loads")... Or because of the lowering of your Vibrational, Energetic level.

It is important to be aware of any signs or signals that may arise. Take a moment to evaluate and analyze these subtle **Energetic aspects** before taking any action. Consider using the "SCAN" method as a first step.

In this way, you are primarily concerned with YOU being and feeling **WELL**. By not doing this, you risk feeling bad after a while. As a consequence, the suffering and pain will occur as a result of the respective negative energies that occur at some point.

By becoming aware of and considering the situations and experiences you encounter in life from an **ENERGETICALLY** (first of all) point of view, you will begin more and more to set yourself **to SEE the subtle ("invisible") side of life**. You will start step by step, to perceive, to be able to detect, "see," "feel," as well, even **the Energetic, Vibrational Frequencies aspects of life.**

It's important to consider them and work with them all to improve your life more and more.

This is the way; this is the path towards a harmonious quality life, including for your spiritual evolution.

Also, this is the way for each of you to fulfill that "personal mission" for which you were born, for which you came to this Planet. The so-called: "**Vision before Birth.**"

In conclusion, **the Choices** you make in your life, Consciously or In-Consciously (Subconsciously), determine both your Health and your life in general.

Your Health is the most essential aspect of your life.

But unfortunately, you come to sense this very well, automatically and directly, often only in that situation when you get a health problem. When you start to suffer, it starts to hurt. In those moments of suffering, your body gets your attention and reminds you about the **Priorities YOU** have in this life. And is communicate you to let go of those nonessential things (for YOUR life and YOUR Personal Evolution) that others around you have directed you towards, or they "programmed" you how to do or how to be...

It is essential for you, as a woman, to become SELF-sufficient and independent, to develop and follow **YOUR OWN Intuition!**... And to follow **YOUR OWN Path** in this life. Especially you to succeed in accomplishing that "some-thing" (that "mission" of YOUR Soul, perhaps) for which you came here in this life.

Another aspect, which it is good to start studying more and to take into account in your life, is:

The presence of Energy and Subtle Fields in ALL that surrounds you.

Things and aspects that directly influence both your health and your life. They manifest anyway, by themselves, whether you believe it or not.

Therefore, please **make wise CHOICES in your life... based first and foremost on YOUR OWN** Intuition.

"Be aware of your thoughts, they become your words;

Be aware of your words, they become your actions;

Be aware of your actions, they become your habits;

Be aware of your habits, they become your character;

Be aware of your character, it becomes your destiny."

- Lao Tzu

"If you want to know the secrets of the Universe, think in terms of Energy, Frequency and Vibration."

- Nikola Tesla

"The important thing is not to acquire, but to discover!

It is not discovering that is important, but how you discover!

The important thing is not how you discover, but what the discovery changes inside you!

What is important is not what it changes within you, but what is changing in others by the fact that something has changed inside you!"

- Tao Teachings

Have a smooth and harmonious journey and a way of light!

Content:

Follow for more books from the guidebooks series:

"Woman Elevate"

www.ingramcontent.com/pod-product-compliance
Lightning Source LLC
Chambersburg PA
CBHW050530160726
48003CB00002B/529